## At Issue

# Are Players' Unions Good for Professional Sports Leagues?

# Other Books in the At Issue Series:

# At Issue

# Are Players' Unions Good for Professional Sports Leagues?

*Thomas Riggs and Company, Book Editor*

**GREENHAVEN PRESS**
*A part of Gale, Cengage Learning*

GALE
CENGAGE Learning·

Detroit • New York • San Francisco • New Haven, Conn • Waterville, Maine • London

GALE
CENGAGE Learning·

Elizabeth Des Chenes, *Director, Publishing Solutions*

© 2013 Greenhaven Press, a part of Gale, Cengage Learning

*For more information, contact:*
Greenhaven Press
27500 Drake Rd.
Farmington Hills, MI 48331-3535
Or you can visit our Internet site at gale.cengage.com

For product information and technology assistance, contact us at

Gale Customer Support, 1-800-877-4253
For permission to use material from this text or product, submit all requests online at
www.cengage.com/permissions

Further permissions questions can be emailed to permissionrequest@cengage.com

Cover image © GStar.

**LIBRARY OF CONGRESS CATALOGING-IN-PUBLICATION DATA**

Are players' unions good for professional sports leagues? / Thomas Riggs and company, book editor.
    p. cm. -- (At issue)
    Summary: "Are Players' Unions Good for Professional Sports Leagues?: Books in this anthology series focus a wide range of viewpoints onto a single controversial issue, providing in-depth discussions by leading advocates, a quick grounding in the issues, and a challenge to critical thinking skills"-- Provided by publisher.
    Includes bibliographical references and index.
    ISBN 978-0-7377-6416-1 (hardback) -- ISBN 978-0-7377-6417-8 (paperback)
    1. Professional sports--Economic aspects--United States--Juvenile literature. 2. Professional sports contracts--United States--Juvenile literature. 3. Professional sports--Law and legislation--United States--Juvenile literature. 4. Collective bargaining--Sports--United States--Juvenile literature. 5. Athletes--Labor unions--United States--Juvenile literature. I. Riggs, Thomas, 1963-
    GV716.A73 2012
    338.4'7796--dc23
                                                              2012025356

Printed in the United States of America
1 2 3 4 5 6 7 16 15 14 13 12

# Contents

# Introduction

The four biggest professional sports leagues in the United States—the National Football League (NFL), National Basketball Association (NBA), Major League Baseball (MLB), and the National Hockey League (NHL)—accrue around $23 billion in revenue each year. Even during the so-called Great Recession, a severe economic downturn that began in late 2007, spectator sports remained among the few industries with regular growth. Inevitably, such success spawns intense debate between athletes and owners over how to distribute profits: players feel that their unique talents and relative celebrity entitle them to a larger share of the wealth, while owners argue that, since they are responsible for any financial losses the teams may suffer, they are also deserving of the majority of the profits. Athletes also contend that they should be allowed to play for any team they choose—that is, for the highest bidder or for the team closest to winning a championship. Owners, on the other hand, largely support measures such as salary caps—limits on the total amount of money a team can spend on its players' salaries—or special designations that keep exceptionally talented players from leaving for a larger market or more successful team.

Professional athletes have long recognized that, as individuals, they stand little chance of winning a legal battle against wealthy and powerful team owners and the league offices that represent them. In certain sports leagues, athletes have opted to protect their interests by organizing themselves into unions, like workers in other industries. The first sports union was formed in 1885 when a small group of National League baseball players led by John Montgomery Ward organized the Brotherhood of Professional Baseball Players. They spoke out against extremely low wages and binding contracts that forbade them from playing for other teams, with Ward famously pronouncing that "players have been bought, sold and exchanged as though they were sheep instead of American citizens." Today, professional athletes in the four major American sports are represented by powerful unions: the Major League Baseball Players Association (MLBPA) formed in 1953, the National Basketball Players Association (NBPA) in 1954, the National Football League Players Association (NFLPA) in 1956, and the National Hockey League Players' Association (NHLPA) in 1967.

Players' unions and team owners regularly negotiate league-wide rules concerning a variety of issues, including profit sharing, player conduct, scheduling, trade restrictions, and the league's responsibility for maintaining players' health and safety during and after their careers. The resulting agreements, known as collective bargaining agreements (CBAs), typically expire after a set number of years determined during negotiations. When a CBA expires, the negotiating process begins again. Collective bargaining sessions can become contentious affairs, with players and owners presenting wildly disparate lists of demands and accusing one another of negotiating in bad faith. In some cases, the two sides are unable to reach an agreement in time for the upcoming season and one of two work-stoppage scenarios occurs: either the owners walk away from negotiations and enforce a "lockout," banning all employees from engaging in league-related activities, or the players end negotiations and engage in a strike. There have been three strikes in the NFL (1974, 1982, and 1987), five in MLB (1972, 1980, 1981, 1985, 1994), and one in the NHL (1992). Lockouts have occurred once in the NFL (2011), four times in the NBA (1995, 1996, 1998, 2011), three times in MLB (1973, 1976, 1990), and twice in the NHL (1994 and 2004). The 2004 NHL lockout was the first work stoppage in American pro sports to cost players and fans an entire season of games.

While team owners and league management would certainly prefer not to have to negotiate with players' unions, their engagement in collective bargaining saves three of the four major sports leagues from being sued for monopolistic practices under the Sherman Antitrust Act of 1890. If athletes decertify their union and renounce their right to collective bargaining, the NFL, NBA, and NHL are all subject to antitrust litigation. Baseball enjoys a blanket exemption from federal antitrust laws under a controversial 1922 Supreme Court ruling, *Federal Baseball Club of Baltimore, Inc. v. National League of Professional Baseball Clubs*. Although the players are not guaranteed to win their antitrust cases and stand the chance of forfeiting their salary for the duration of the lockout, the threat of a protracted court procedure and the high cost of penalties associated with antitrust violations usually force owners to return to the negotiating table and reach a settlement with players for a new CBA. This was the case in the early 1990s when the NFLPA decertified and filed a number of antitrust lawsuits against the NFL—most notably *Freeman McNeil et al. v. National Football League*—and eventually compelled the league to make a number of concessions in the 1993 CBA. In 2010 the Supreme Court rejected a request from the NFL to grant the league an antitrust exemption similar to what baseball has, thereby setting the stage for future antitrust litigation.

In 2011 both the NFL and the NBA experienced work stoppages. In the NFL, the players' union and the owners disagreed over how to divide the league's $9 billion in revenue, and the owners imposed a lockout beginning on March 11. The union responded by decertifying, and a group of high-profile players, including quarterbacks Tom Brady, Drew Brees, and Peyton Manning, filed antitrust suits against the league. The suits, Manning claims, were intended to have a twofold effect: "First, to show unified strength on behalf of benefiting all players; second, to see a resolution that recognizes the interests of players and management." The NFL quickly sought to reach a settlement with the players, and the lockout officially ended when the NFLPA re-formed and the two sides signed a ten-year CBA in August 2011. The NBA experienced similar labor strife, as the owners imposed a lockout on July 1 and cancelled several weeks of the season (along with player paychecks for that period) before the players voted to dissolve the NBPA and filed two antitrust lawsuits against the league on November 17. The owners promptly returned to the negotiating table, and both sides signed a ten-year CBA in December, leading to a shortened season of 66 rather than 82 games per team.

Sports fans and commentators react to work stoppages in a number of ways. Some side with the owners and claim that players, whose salaries range in the millions of dollars, should be satisfied playing a game they purportedly love for more money than most people will earn in a lifetime. Others back the players and accuse owners of exploiting athletes, whose talents are what make sports leagues so popular and financially successful. Perhaps the most common response is to view sports labor strife as a money-grab between two already wealthy groups, one that needlessly threatens the livelihood of thousands of middle-class stadium workers, ticket sellers, and local businesses near the various stadiums. As the following viewpoints show, the arguments surrounding sports labor disputes often evolve into a broader debate over the role that unions play in American society and are rife with implications concerning the state of employer/employee relations throughout the United States.

# 1

# Players' Unions Make Professional Sports More Competitive and Fair

*Timothy L. Epstein*

*Timothy L. Epstein is a partner in the law firm of SmithAmundsen, where he is chair of the sports law practice group. He is also an adjunct professor at Loyola University Chicago School of Law, where he teaches courses in sports law.*

*Players' unions are good for American professional sports. By allowing athletes to collectively bargain for certain regulations instead of having league officials determine the rules for player salaries, player movement, and the like, American sports leagues ensure greater equality of competition between teams. In Europe, where players do not enjoy collective bargaining and teams are free to offer virtually any kind of contract they choose to individual players, only a few select—and wealthy—teams win championships. In the United States, however, collective bargaining has provided incentives for star players to remain in smaller markets, and it gives hope to sports fans all over the country that their team will one day win it all.*

With the NBA and the NFL labor disputes making front page headlines this summer [2011] and our historical sports landscape littered with strikes, lockouts and work stoppages, one cannot help but wonder: Would our sports leagues be better off without unionized players' associations and collective bargaining? After all, from a fan's perspective, a dispute pitting billionaires against millionaires hardly induces sympathy and disenchantment is certainly merited.

Yet, while these lockouts might cause games to be missed and dollars to be forfeited, the mechanisms causing short term losses are beneficial in the long run, and promote the most essential element of sport: competition. The structure of labor law in this country is fundamental and it fosters this on-field competition through the bilateral imposition of conditions that ordinarily would not be tolerable in a free market system.

---

*Courts have recognized that competition in the free market is not always conducive to on-field competition.*

---

## North American Restrictions

All four major sports leagues in North America have players' unions and teams operate within systems controlled by various bargained for restraints such as age restrictions, salary caps and entry drafts. Conversely, European sports leagues are structured differently and operate in a system that is much less restrictive. Player movement is almost completely vulnerable to the free market. In Europe, there are no players' unions and leagues are governed by overarching governing bodies such as Union des Associations Europeennes de Football (UEFA), which governs European football (i.e. soccer). There are no entry drafts, clubs are free to sign players at any age and there is no cap on salaries. The aggregate effect of this system has spawned a top-heavy structure manifesting that free market competition does not necessarily equate to on-field "competition."

In the United States, many of the constraints under which leagues operate do not pass antitrust muster under Section

One of the Sherman Act. Section One of the Sherman Act states, "Every contract, combination . . . or conspiracy, in restraint of trade or commerce . . . is hereby declared to be illegal." Restraints such as age restrictions, salary caps and entry drafts would all likely be considered per se illegal under the Sherman Act, or at minimum, proscribed under rule of reason analysis because the restraints limit players' rights to be compensated freely and limit players' market access.

Because of these restrictions, labor unions are essential. Courts have carved out nonstatutory labor exemptions for restraints that would otherwise be considered illegal, as long as such restraints are collectively bargained for. Interestingly, sports leagues have often been a battleground for the tension between antitrust law and labor law. Courts have recognized that competition in the free market is not always conducive to on-field competition and that certain restrictions actually improve the product in the professional sports context.

In *Mackey v. National Football League*, the 8th Circuit articulated a three-factor test to determine if a restriction is subject to a non-statutory labor exemption. The exemption may be applied when a restraint on trade: 1) involves mandatory subjects of bargaining; 2) primarily affects the parties involved; and 3) is reached through bona fide arm's length dealing.

The *Mackey* court struck down the NFL's "Rozelle Rule," which required teams that acquired a player whose contract had expired to compensate the player's former team. The court held that the rule violated the third prong of the test because the rule was unilaterally instituted and was not agreed upon through bona fide arm's length dealing.

## Fewer Regulations in Europe

By contrast, there is no such labor exemption in Europe, and even if there were, athletes are not unionized. This leaves sports leagues and the unilaterally imposed regulatory schemes susceptible to attack under European competition law. In Europe, Article 81 of the Treaty Establishing the European Community applies to competition law. Article 81(1) prohibits agreements that prevent, restrict or distort competition either by object or effect. Article 81(3) permits exemptions to Article 81(1), but the restrictions must be indispensable to the market efficiencies created.

---

*The free market system in Europe is actually detrimental to competition.*

---

The sporting world in Europe has also been used as a battleground for the fight between labor law and antitrust law. In 1995, the European Court of Justice made a clear statement regarding the European Commission's disfavor of market restraints. The court's seminal ruling in *Union Royale Belge des Societes de Football Association ASBL v. Bosman* had two important holdings: 1) transfer fees for players who are out of contract are illegal; and 2) a quota system limiting the number of foreign players on teams' rosters was illegal.

The *Bosman* ruling has had profound effects. These restrictions benefited smaller clubs by regulating player movement and maintaining balance. The transfer system was first implemented for this very purpose. It helped the smaller clubs maintain their star players and at least allowed the smaller clubs to gain revenue if these clubs did lose players. Now, though some restrictions remain, player movement has been liberalized and it has become increasingly difficult for these smaller clubs to retain, let alone obtain, the best players. Players can now demand higher wages more commensurate with their market value, and oftentimes only the wealthiest clubs can afford these salaries.

In basketball, this free market is allowing the wealthiest European clubs to sign American stars such as Deron Williams while the NBA is entrenched in what looks to be a prolonged lockout. Certainly only the richest European teams will be able to entice NBA superstars. If European teams were subject to the same restrictions as American teams, these players would potentially be forced to enter into a draft, and teams could not lure them in with astronomical salaries.

## A Lack of Competitive Balance

Empirical evidence supports the contention that the free market system in Europe is actually detrimental to competition. In the English Premiere League, the triumvirate of Manchester United, Chelsea and Arsenal have won every title since 1995. The same holds true in the Spanish League, where Real Madrid and FC Barcelona dominate; as well as the Italian League, where Juventus, AC Milan and Inter Milan reign. These clubs are free to outspend the competition to bring in the best players regardless of age or nationality, which creates more revenue and ultimately broadens the chasm between the have's and have not's. In stark contrast, the NFL has had 12 different Super Bowl champions since 1995.

This lack of competitive balance in European football is well documented. There has been a recent movement toward implementing some sort of salary cap in European football, but this would likely be subject to Article 81(1) of the EC Treaty because it would restrict or distort competition, and thus would have to satisfy the exception requirements of Article 81(3). This would be a difficult hurdle to overcome and would require showing that European football would be at risk of existence because of inadequate competition.

Interestingly, Article 81 could pose a significant hurdle if North American sports leagues choose to expand overseas, which has been discussed as part of leagues' globalization strategies. North American leagues would likely be subject to strict European competition law and many player movement restrictions could be in jeopardy.

The significance of labor unions and the nonstatutory labor exemption is clear from this comparison of the American and European systems of sport. As long as restrictions on player movement are agreed upon by the leagues and the players' unions, the conditions will not face the intense antitrust scrutiny that a potential salary cap would endure in Europe. Many of the same restrictions that are covered by the nonstatutory labor exemption in the United States would be illegal within this European framework. Much of what makes our sports leagues in the United States so competitive are these rules that regulate player movement. The absence of players' unions and the interjection of European courts has clearly hindered the competitive balance.

Sports fans watch games because of the competition and maintain perpetual hope that one day their team will eventually win the championship. Every spring, Cubs fans utter, "this is our year." In America, this rhetoric is not empty and optimism is not lost because our leagues and courts have developed a system that brings parity and gives teams a fighting chance. In most cases, belief in one's team is not completely delusional. By contrast, for fans of many European sports teams, such hope teeters on the edge of utter fantasy. While sports leagues' labor disputes are aggravating and the thought of games being lost is disheartening, ultimately, collective bargaining through players' unions preserves the integrity of sporting competition in America.

# 2

# Players' Unions Make Professional Sports Too Expensive for Fans

*Ben Shapiro*

*Ben Shapiro is a conservative political commentator and the author of such books as* Primetime Propaganda: The True Hollywood Story of How the Left Took Over Your TV.

*Players' unions are to blame for the rising costs of professional sports events and the frequent interruptions caused by labor disputes. Because team owners risk losing a great deal of wealth by purchasing sports teams, and the players themselves are at no risk of missing paychecks even when they do not perform as expected, the owners should be free to stipulate the terms of players' contracts however they see fit. NBA owners in particular have made far too many concessions to the players' union, and these compromises have driven up prices on everything from tickets, to parking, to snacks. Owners should instead draw a hard line and refuse to negotiate with the union.*

This year [2011], we may not get to see Kobe Bryant of the Los Angeles Lakers play. The people of Italy probably will. While the National Basketball Association lockout continues, Bryant is considering a deal worth $5 million for one year from the Virtus Bologna. He's not the only NBA player who might appear overseas. Deron Williams of the New Jersey Nets signed a contract with the Turkish team Besiktas, worth $200,000 per month. Many more top players are jumping overseas during the work stoppage.

By contrast, Bryant signed a contract on April 2, 2010, with the Lakers for $87 million, which means he's playing for about one-sixth what he would be if the NBA lockout ended. Williams has a player option for $17.7 million next year, so he's playing for about one-seventh his normal pay.

So why are these players not on the court in the United States?

Thanks to the NBA Players' Union. That's also the reason you pay such high prices at the ticket office and can only afford seats in the third tier. It's why a beer costs $7 at these games. And it's why so many of the players are spoiled brats.

The current [2011] NBA lockout pits the owners, the folks who risk their capital, against the players, who risk no capital, who have guaranteed contracts and who hardly lack for pay. (The average NBA yearly salary is $3.4 million.) This isn't Norma Rae [the title character of a 1979 film about a factory worker who forms a union]. It's a monopolistic shakedown.

---

*What business owner gives his employees a percentage of the gross, before expenses?*

---

## Issues Leading to the Lockout

So what are the issues that prompted the lockout? The current collective bargaining agreement expires in this year. Supposedly, the players want more intra-team revenue sharing, which makes sense from their perspective—if small market teams have more cash, they can jack up the bidding on players. But revenue sharing should be a question between the owners. The players should have no part of that negotiation, since it is the owners' cash.

The players also want to prevent a luxury tax imposed by the owners on themselves to prevent certain teams (read: the Lakers) from doing a New York Yankees and stockpiling talent and creating competitive imbalances. Again, this is not the players' business. If owners want to impose a tax on themselves, that is their business, since it is the owners' money.

The players currently receive 51 percent of the gross revenue garnered by the teams. This is an insanely stupid deal the owners never should have done. After all, what business owner gives his employees a percentage of the gross, before expenses? And the players are complaining about it. The teams lost a combined $370 million last season, and it's not hard to see why. A typical team may take in about $20 million in gate receipts (that's the actual stat for the Milwaukee Bucks, for example). They pay out three times that at least just in salary for their players (the Bucks spent $69 million in 2010). They make up revenue from advertising and TV contracts and all the rest, but NBA players are hardly being paid poorly. Again, the gross revenue shouldn't be any of the players' business, because it is the owners' capital.

---

*Members of the NBA Players Union are grabbing for a chunk of something that isn't theirs in the first place.*

---

Because of all of this, the owners are pushing for a hard salary cap, meaning that no team can spend more than a certain amount. The players don't want this, with good reason. But again, it's the owners' call, since it is the owners who pay.

The teams also want to apply a personal conduct policy to the league, to prevent idiots like Gilbert Arenas from bringing loaded handguns into locker rooms. The players oppose this because they want to continue to be able to act like morons without losing their jobs. Could you do this at your job and keep it? Didn't think so.

## Increased Costs Are Passed on to the Consumers

The bottom line: Members of the NBA Players Union are grabbing for a chunk of something that isn't theirs in the first place. And that's what players unions have been doing in every sport, driving up the cost of business—costs that are passed on to the consumer. It now costs almost $50 for an average NBA ticket. That's been steady since 1999, when the players and owners locked out. Between 1990 and 1999, the ticket prices—prompted by players' demands, which forced another lockout in 1995—rose 108.1 percent.

What about owners who bargain collectively? They're all in the same business, so they're more like franchisees of McDonald's than owners of Burger King vs. owners of McDonald's. They don't compete with each other because their business has common ground rules. That's why if they were smart (which they aren't), they'd tell the players to shove it. If they don't like the deal, they can find work elsewhere. They'd have to wait a couple of years to do that, though, until the current contracts expire.

But they're not smart, so they'll likely come to some sort of arrangement. And the fans will pay higher prices. Eventually, however, we'll stop going to the games. Then both the owners and the players will see where the true power lies: with the consumer.

# 3

# Football's Future If the Players Win

*Roger Goodell*

*Roger Goodell is the commissioner of the National Football League. He has a degree in economics from Washington & Jefferson College and has worked in the NFL league office since 1982. He was elected commissioner by NFL team owners in 2006.*

*The NFL players' union has provided numerous benefits for the NFL and its fans. Through collective bargaining, it has increased player compensation, allowed the league to add teams, and ensured competitive balance. The players' tactic of dissolving the union—allowing them to file individual lawsuits against the league—will ensure that all of these gains are lost, leading to an unbalanced league where superstars and major-market teams reap the majority of benefits.*

Late Monday afternoon, U.S. District Court Judge Susan Richard Nelson issued a ruling that may significantly alter professional football as we know it.

For six weeks, there has been a work stoppage in the National Football League as the league has sought to negotiate a new collective-bargaining agreement with the players. But Judge Nelson ordered the end of the stoppage and recognized the players' right to dissolve their union. By blessing this negotiating tactic, the decision may endanger one of the most popular and successful sports leagues in history.

What would the NFL look like without a collectively bar-gained compromise? For many years, the collectively bargained system—which has given the players union enhanced free agency and capped the amount that owners spend on salaries—has worked enormously well for the NFL, for NFL players, and for NFL fans.

For players, the system allowed player compensation to skyrocket—pay and benefits doubled in the last 10 years alone. The system also offered players comparable economic opportunities throughout the league, from Green Bay and New Orleans to San Francisco and New York. In addition, it fostered conditions that allowed the NFL to expand by four teams, extending careers and creating jobs for hundreds of additional players.

---

*A union victory threatens to overturn the carefully constructed system of competitive balance that makes NFL games and championship races so unpredictable and exciting.*

---

For clubs and fans, the trade-off afforded each team a genuine opportunity to compete for the Super Bowl, greater cost certainty, and incentives to invest in the game. Those incentives translated into two dozen new and renovated stadiums and technological innovations such as the NFL Network and nfl.com.

Under the union lawyers' plan, reflected in the complaint that they filed in federal court, the NFL would be forced to operate in a dramatically different way. To be sure, their approach would benefit some star players and their agents (and, of course, the lawyers themselves). But virtually everyone else—including the vast majority of players as well as the fans—would suffer.

Rather than address the challenge of improving the collective-bargaining agreement for the benefit of the game, the union-financed lawsuit attacks virtually every aspect of the current system including the draft, the salary cap and free-agency rules, which collectively have been responsible for the quality and popularity of the game for nearly two decades. A union victory threatens to overturn the carefully constructed system of competitive balance that makes NFL games and championship races so unpredictable and exciting.

---

*Under this vision, players and fans would have none of the protections or benefits that only a union . . . can deliver.*

---

In the union lawyers' world, every player would enter the league as an unrestricted free agent, an independent contractor free to sell his services to any team. Every player would again become an unrestricted free agent each time his contract expired. And each team would be free to spend as much or as little as it wanted on player payroll or on an individual player's compensation.

Any league-wide rule relating to terms of player employment would be subject to antitrust challenge in courts throughout the country. Any player could sue—on his own behalf or representing a class—to challenge any league rule that he believes unreasonably restricts the "market" for his services.

Under this vision, players and fans would have none of the protections or benefits that only a union (through a collective-bargaining agreement) can deliver. What are the potential ramifications for players, teams, and fans? Here are some examples:

- *No draft.* "Why should there even be a draft?" said player agent Brian Ayrault. "Players should be able to choose who they work for. Markets should determine the value of all contracts. Competitive balance is a fallacy."

- *No minimum team payroll.* Some teams could have $200 million payrolls while others spend $50 million or less.

- *No minimum player salary.* Many players could earn substantially less than today's minimums.

- *No standard guarantee to compensate players who suffer season- or career-ending injuries.* Players would instead negotiate whatever compensation they could.

- *No league-wide agreements on benefits.* The generous benefit programs now available to players throughout the league would become a matter of individual club choice and individual player negotiation.

- *No limits on free agency.* Players and agents would team up to direct top players to a handful of elite teams. Other teams, perpetually out of the running for the playoffs, would serve essentially as farm teams for the elites.

- *No league-wide rule limiting the length of training camp or required off-season workout obligations.* Each club would have its own policies.

- *No league-wide testing program for drugs of abuse or performance enhancing substances.* Each club could have its own program—or not.

Any league-wide agreement on these subjects would be the subject of antitrust challenge by any player who asserted that he had been "injured" by the policy or whose lawyer perceived an opportunity to bring attention to his client or himself. Some such agreements might survive antitrust scrutiny, but the prospect of litigation would inhibit league-wide agreements with respect to most, if not all, of these subjects.

In an environment where they are essentially independent contractors, many players would likely lose significant benefits and other protections previously provided on a collective basis as part of the union-negotiated collective-bargaining agreement. And the prospect of improved benefits for retired players would be nil.

Is this the NFL that players want? A league where elite players attract enormous compensation and benefits while other players—those lacking the glamour and bargaining power of the stars—play for less money, fewer benefits and shorter careers than they have today? A league where the competitive ability of teams in smaller communities (Buffalo, New Orleans, Green Bay and others) is forever cast into doubt by blind adherence to free-market principles that favor teams in larger, better-situated markets?

Prior to filing their litigation, players and their representatives publicly praised the current system and argued for extending the status quo. Now they are singing a far different tune, attacking in the courts the very arrangements they said were working just fine.

Is this the NFL that fans want? A league where carefully constructed rules proven to generate competitive balance—close and exciting games every Sunday and close and exciting divisional and championship contests—are cast aside? Do the players and their lawyers have so little regard for the fans that they think this really serves their interests?

These outcomes are inevitable under any approach other than a comprehensive collective-bargaining agreement. That is especially true of an approach that depends on litigation settlements negotiated by lawyers. But that is what the players' attorneys are fighting for in court. And that is what will be at stake as the NFL appeals Judge Nelson's ruling to the Eighth Circuit Court of Appeals.

# 4

# Players' Unions Protect Owners, Not Players or Fans

*Arn Tellem*

*Arn Tellem is a sports agent who represents professional basketball and baseball players.*

*Players' unions have outlived their purpose because team owners have discovered a negotiating tactic that effectively neutralizes unions' bargaining power. In previous years, players' unions worked to establish minimum standards for the treatment of all players, but recently they have been drawn into debates over the maximum salaries for a select few superstars, thereby allowing owners to blame labor disputes on highly paid players. Because the unions have been complicit in numerous concessions made to owners in recent decades, the players should dissolve the union and sue the league as individuals, a tactic that would likely force the owners to settle out of court to avoid a lengthy and expensive trial.*

Having grown up during the New Deal [a series of economic programs implemented by the US government during the Great Depression], my parents made me keenly aware that unions gave workers what they lacked individually—a voice. My childhood hero was Marvin Miller, the labor economist who in 1968 negotiated the Major League Baseball Players Association's first collective bargaining agreement with team owners. Miller's own new deal raised the minimum salary to $10,000 from $6,000, the first increase since the 1940s. (It's now $414,000.)

Miller introduced the concept of salary arbitration, fought for stronger pensions and encouraged ballplayers to challenge the owners who, wielding the reserve clause, routinely treated players like chattel. The clause effectively bound players to one team in perpetuity at that team's discretion. With Miller at the helm, the reserve clause was abolished in 1975, paving the way for free agency.

---

*The N.F.L. and N.B.A. players consistently allow the owners to define the issues. More often than not, management gets the concessions it seeks.*

---

Thirty-six years later, I wonder if unions in professional sports other than baseball have outlived their purpose. Pro football players voted to decertify their union in March immediately before the owners imposed a long-expected lockout. Faced with a similar situation, pro basketball players will almost certainly follow suit. As a player agent who represents 45 N.B.A. players, I think they should the moment the current season ends.

## Collective Bargaining Is Ineffectual

In the N.F.L. and the N.B.A., the noble ideal of solidarity has played itself out. Collective bargaining has proved ineffectual in protecting the rights of football and basketball players. The most that their union leaders can hope for is to minimize concessions. Enhancements to wages, benefits and working conditions are no longer even discussed. Meanwhile, team owners have set bargaining goals well beyond their needs and then demanded more than they could ever hope to achieve.

When the union inevitably balks, the owners feign indignation, complaining that the players won't compromise even though compromising would play into the owners' hands. Inevitably, the leagues' overreach achieves its desired effect, preventing the unions from advancing the players' legitimate concerns. The N.F.L. and N.B.A. players consistently allow the owners to define the issues. More often than not, management gets the concessions it seeks.

Pro football, the most profitable sport in the world, cries hard times and demands a longer schedule, a shrinking salary cap and a rookie scale that would include limits on length of contracts and guaranteed money. Team owners—who slice $1 billion out of the N.F.L.'s annual $9 billion pie before the remaining revenue is divided with the players—kicked off negotiations by insisting on an additional $1.3 billion a year for the next decade. The union countered by offering $550 million over four years without asking for financial verification. Today, the sides remain hundreds of millions of dollars a year apart.

Miller believed that a union should set minimum standards, not maximum salaries. Of the four major unions in pro sports, baseball's is the only one that has successfully pushed back management on this issue. (In 1999, the N.B.A.'s union agreed to a salary cap for individual players.) Interestingly, no commissioner, team executive or coach has a compensation cap. Nor have they been asked to take pay cuts despite the league's supposed financial troubles. Perhaps most tellingly, no owners have limits on the amount their clubs can appreciate in value.

---

*Rather than compete in a free market, management has exploited the weaknesses of unions to inhibit competition.*

---

Despite unparalleled revenue, the salaries of N.F.L. players are significantly lower than that of their counterparts in baseball and basketball. Football is the team sport with the shortest careers, averaging 3.5 years, and without the guaranteed contracts common in the other two.

Rather than address this reality, the N.F.L. wants to expand its schedule, which will no doubt result in more injuries, possibly more serious ones. Even more unconscionably, after an N.F.L. player leaves the game, he's entitled to only five years of health insurance. In such a brutal sport, adequate and permanent health care should be a given.

## The Unions Have Allowed Collusion

For years, the N.F.L. and the N.B.A. have found their players associations to be unwitting partners. Rather than compete in a free market, management has exploited the weaknesses of unions to inhibit competition. By shielding owners from the scrutiny of antitrust laws, the unions have effectively allowed collusion. More often than not, the result has been union retreat—on salary caps, salary scales and taxes.

Decertification has allowed N.F.L. players to sue the league on antitrust grounds, and could eventually force owners to open their books to scrutiny if the case proceeds. At the very least decertification allowed the players to get an injunction from a federal judge to stop the lockout, pending an appeal. Sure, the N.F.L. could attempt to impose whatever salary and free-agency restrictions it wishes, but it will have to tread carefully. If the league loses an antitrust suit, it will have to pay each player affected three times his actual economic loss.

Is it any wonder that N.F.L. and N.B.A. executives bewail decertification, and insist that agreements be reached through negotiation? The sad irony is that without a union, the courts and antitrust laws will level the playing field so that the risk is not borne solely by the players. Given the considerable risk of going to trial, the league commissioners will probably get what they want: a settlement negotiated by lawyers.

Something is fundamentally wrong when the only effective weapon in a union's arsenal is dissolution. The hard-won early victories—health benefits, minimum wage—have been over-shadowed by the sacrifices that players are now not just asked, but also expected to make.

# 5

# Agents, Not Unions, Are the Cause of NBA Labor Strife

*Kevin Ding*

*Kevin Ding is a sports reporter for the* Orange County Register.

*While neither the players nor the owners held defensible posi-tions in the 2011 National Basketball Association (NBA) lock-out, the true culprit of such labor strife is the greed of player agents. The salary concessions demanded by NBA owners would not meaningfully reduce the salary of the average player, but they would significantly diminish the income of the agents, which is based on the total compensation paid to the entire roster of talent that they represent. Thus, agents such as Arn Tellem en-danger entire seasons by arguing for such drastic measures as the dissolution of players' unions in order to maximize their own potential profits.*

The NBA already took the action of the most open-faced, high-flying game in the world from America's hardwood into hotel conference rooms for collective bargaining tedium.

With the filing of two antitrust lawsuits by NBA players Tuesday in U.S. District Court, the scene shifts again—and the trash talking will now have be done in Latin. Dockets and motions and files . . . oh, my.

NBA action, it's . . . been lawyered!

And old dudes in suits in bad lighting isn't quite going to compete with [football players] Aaron Rodgers and Calvin Johnson in HD.

While it is universally understood that "football is king," and interest in the NBA doesn't peak till after Christmas, a study offers some interesting context about just what the NBA could be costing itself with this long lockout.

Using online research tools to calculate the percentage of media attention devoted to each professional sport in 2010, HighBeam Research pegs the NFL (28.1 percent) barely ahead of the NBA (26.8) . . . and far ahead of the NHL (15.6), PGA (12.1), NASCAR (7.9) and Major League Baseball (5.9—ouch). The NBA was within two percentage points of the NFL in 2008 and '09, too.

The NFL, however, handled its lockout this year without any collateral damage. The NBA is shooting itself in the head.

Maybe the NBA's marketers just need to spin it a little better to make it interesting to the public: Black people vs. white people! Lonely player groupies are people, too! Rich people unhappy! Kobe [Bryant] unhappy! LeBron [James] unhappy!

---

*If not for the faction of agents pushing their agenda instead of helping union leaders with theirs, this deal could've been done long ago.*

---

## Playing the Blame Game

But there are too few likable characters here to make this thing watchable. It's almost too easy to play the blame game:

The bullying owners overplayed their hand in pursuit of certain profits being handed to them; the players were out of touch with our economic reality. Done and done. Anyone writing about both epic fails is making a lot of sense but stating the rather obvious. Anyone who would disagree with either statement must be a blood relative of an NBA player or owner.

But if you were to play this out as a drama, the guys who would also evoke deep hostility would be the creepy, crawly player agents—even though they've receded into the background now that the players' union undercut certain agents' grand plan for decertification by disclaiming interest Monday and dissolving that way. Agents are always key sources for reporters, so it's understandable they haven't faced much media criticism, but it needs to be said.

Union president Derek Fisher isn't in any position to claim any victories, but remember back in September how he wrote plainly about the meddling agents in a letter to the players: "It is because they have not come to me once that I question their motives."

If not for the faction of agents pushing their agenda instead of helping union leaders with theirs, this deal could've been done long ago. To be fair, if the union had decertified from the start, as many agents advocated doing without ever negotiating in good faith, maybe this deal could've been done by now via settlement also. But decertification wasn't the path that was chosen—and now here the players are at this late date, filing papers in the courtroom instead of taking the court.

---

*The agents were doing their own money grab this offseason.*

---

To understand why prominent agents such as Mark Bartelstein, Bill Duffy, Dan Fegen, Jeff Schwartz and Arn Tellem have been so frantic over the players' concessions to the owners in collective bargaining can be revealed through some quick, eye-opening math:

Seeing 2 percent of the much-discussed Basketball Related Income [BRI] go the owners' way instead of the players' way wouldn't really do much to the average player, whose $5.15 million salary would become $4.96 million. (That's $80 million for two BRI points, 430 total NBA players, $186,000 each.)

But if you take that $186,000 lost and multiply it by 27 player clients (the average that the aforementioned five agents represent) and then count the agent's 3 percent commission (he can take up to 4 percent) and multiply it by 30 years (while the players' average career is less than five years, the agent will be repping players who aren't even born yet) . . . you get *$4 1/2 million* of his own money you could realistically say an agent would lose by conceding that 2 percent of BRI to the owners.

## Agents Act in Self-Interest

It's a crude formula not even factoring in annual growth, but the message should be clear. The agents were doing their own money grab this offseason—and with less reason than anyone to care if it happened to cost everyone the 2011–12 NBA season.

So they stalled the momentum of negotiations more than once, staging all their conference calls with each other and pushing their message on players whose competitive streaks jibe with militant pride. It's undeniably compelling to preach about current players' obligation to fight against greedy owners also for the sake of future players . . . and guess who will be taking commission off those future players?

Agents are usually lawyers, which brings is back to that. Lawyers—as David Stern shows—are outstanding at making arguments and doing so with conviction, which is so often the key to winning any discussion. It's no surprise when so many players turn to their agents for counsel on all their business that they just bought what was being sold all offseason.

Pau Gasol, one of the smartest guys you'll find in any sport, was left Monday spewing erroneous info from his Twitter account—material straight from the decertification playbook ("This doesn't mean that it won't be a season. The union & the league will still have 45 days to get to an agreement before it gets dissolved"), unaware the actual move made was not the agent-pushed decertification. By disclaiming interest, the union introduced totally different rules that don't allow more collective bargaining now.

Gasol's agent, Tellem, . . . wrote back in May [2011] an editorial in *The New York Times* urging NBA players to decertify their union as soon as the season ended to avoid giving concessions to the owners.

Some players were certainly realistic, willing to get informed and wanting to play.

Far too many players simply trusted agents who lack everyone else's understanding for what it really means to grow the game.

# 6

# NBA Labor Issues Are Based in Racism

## David J. Leonard

*David J. Leonard, a professor in the Department of Critical Culture, Gender, and Race Studies at Washington State University, is the author of* After Artest: The NBA and the Assault on Blackness.

*The 2011 NBA lockout reflects the racism inherent in the league's policies and management structure. Recent rule changes that restrict player speech, dress, and other forms of expression are evidence of discomfort among the NBA's mostly white ownership and fan base with the increased wealth and freedom of the primarily black players, and the owners' unwillingness to fairly negotiate with the players suggests that they see this discomfort as a form of leverage. By painting the players as greedy thugs, the owners gain a decided advantage in public perception. The players' union, in response, plays directly into these racist tactics by restricting the players' ability to make public statements concerning labor issues.*

Following an exhibition game in Philadelphia, [sports reporter] Michael Tillery asked the following of [basketball player] Carmelo ["Melo"] Anthony:

> Michael Tillery: Carmelo I don't know if anyone asked you this but the fans are wondering why there isn't such of a . . .

NBA presence . . . NBA players coming out and speaking on this issue (NBA lockout) publicly like in the NFL . . . like in other situations.

Carmelo Anthony: "We're not allowed. We're not allowed. I mean everybody has their own opinion . . . you hear people talk here and there . . . but nobody don't really come out and say what they really want to say. That's just the society we live in. Athletes today are scared to make Muhammad Ali type statements."

Not surprisingly, his comments have led to questions about today's NBA players, their resolve, their commitment, heart, and courage. For example, one blogger offered the following: "What does Carmelo mean by 'we're not allowed'? Who's stopping them? Is Carmelo right? Do you think athletes are punks in the modern era as opposed to the way Muhammad Ali stuck his neck out for Vietnam? Maybe these guys should just man up and make changes!" [Reporter] Kelly Dwyer was similarly dismissive, questioning Anthony's reference to Ali:

Oh, Carmelo. He's not lying. He's not wrong. But comparing Ali's stand against a conflict in Southeastern Asia that had gone terribly wrong to a discussion over the sharing of actual billions of dollars in Basketball Related Income is the absolute height of absurdity. Yes, athletes today are scared to make Muhammad Ali-type statements (as is the case with most people that want to keep their jobs), but the application of an anecdote like that to a situation like the NBA lockout is completely and utterly wrong.

*The lockout represents an attempt to capitalize on the perception of NBA players as thugs, as criminals, as greedy, and undeserving anti-role models.*

While folks in the blogosphere used Melo's comments to incite division and to chastise the union for silencing its members, it would seem that his comments demonstrate the ways that race impacts the lockout while illustrating the potential efforts from the union to manage and mediate the racially based contempt faced by NBA players. As Michael Tillery told me, "The NBA more than any other pro league seems to have an image problem based more on race than anything. You could say the league is more popular when a white player is doing superstar things." As such, you cannot understand these comments outside a larger racial landscape.

## The NBA and Race

To understand Carmelo Anthony's comments require a larger context. His comments (and the lockout itself) are very much tied to the larger history of the NBA and race. For example, in wake of the Palace Brawl [a 2004 fight between players and fans at the Palace, an arena in Michigan], the NBA implemented a series of draconian policies that sought to both appease white fans and corporate sponsors who were increasingly uncomfortable with its racial optics, all while disciplining the players to comply and embody a different sort of blackness. According to Michael Tillery, the brilliant commentator, "Since the Brawl and even going back to Kermit Washington's punch of Rudy Tomjonovich [in 1977], a case could be made that any outspoken player in any regard is influenced to be silenced simply to protect the NBA brand because of an apparent race disconnect."

The owner's intransigent position and demands for a hard cap (although at the time of writing the owners appear to have softened on this position, at least at a surface level), major reduction in player access to league revenues, and a myriad of others positions all seem to reflect a sense of leverage. In other words, the owners seem to be trying to capitalize on the contempt and animosity that has long plagued NBA players, a fact worsened by the assault on blackness that followed the Palace Brawl. In a brilliant interview with Michael Tillery, [basketball player] Ron Artest reflects on the public perception and demonization of NBA players that reflects larger racial animus and ideology: "The NBA is not a thug league. There's a couple of players that grew up similar to rappers who have grown up. What are they going to lynch us for that too? It's not our fault that we grew up that way. We are talented and smart."

The lockout represents an attempt to capitalize on the perception of NBA players as thugs, as criminals, as greedy, and undeserving anti-role models. It appears to be an effort to convert the leverage and power that comes from the narrative and ideological assumptions so often linked to black players into greater financial power for the league's owners.

In thinking about Melo's comments and the overall reticence of players to speak about the current labor situation leaves me thinking that this is a concerted strategy to combat the advantages that the owners possess (the NBA version of a southern strategy [the Republican political strategy of appealing to voters in southern states by exploiting racist fears]). The union is most certainly trying to correct the public relations difficulties that it faced in 1998 (and throughout its history), obstacles that emanate from America's racial landscape.

---

*The NBA lockout ... was about an increasing level of fan animus directed toward the league's primarily black players, much of which reflected the insertion of race into the discussion.*

---

During the last NBA lockout, Kenny Anderson, then a point guard with the Boston Celtics, generated quite a bit of backlash when he announced, "I was thinking about selling one of my cars, I don't need all of them. You know, just get rid of the Mercedes." Fulfilling people's stereotypes about rich and entitled black athletes, Anderson's comments generated little sympathy from fans, amplifying growing resentment toward the NBA's primarily black populace. [Sports reporter] Mike Wise, seemingly mocking Anderson, penned the following:

> Two months after the National Basketball Association's lockout came and his paycheck went, Kenny Anderson began contemplating the unthinkable. It had nothing to do with asking his mother in Queens for his old room back or taking a part-time security job; he figured there were only so many indignities young millionaires should have to face.
>
> But with his penchant for buying what he wanted and his accountant having to borrow against his stocks to keep investing, Anderson realized it might be time to do without. Sort of. . . .
>
> Extravagant and expensive tastes have been a hallmark of young millionaire athletes. But without games and paychecks, N.B.A. players are about to learn the frugal side of living large. How long many of them can cope without a biweekly salary may mean the difference in their economic game of chicken with the owners.

---

*Be visible, play, and even make money but don't dare speak about injustices, inequalities, or the conditions of labor.*

---

Similarly, [retired NBA player] Patrick Ewing, then union president, described the players' predicament in the following way: "If you look at people who play professional sports, not a lot of them are financially secure. They make a lot of money, and they also spend a lot of money." Alonzo Mourning did the unthinkable during the 1998 lockout: he talked about race. "I think there is a perception from the owners to even some fans that we're blacks who should be happy with what we've got, fair or not," he argued. "There's a lack of respect given us in large part because we're athletes. I'm not saying it's all about race because it's not. But it plays a factor." Such statements did not merely turn public opinion to the owners, but did so because the comments were interpreted through dominant white racial frames, undermining player leverage.

## Backlash Against Black Players

So when Alonzo Mourning "inserted" race into the discussion, noting the existence of double standards and how race over-determined media coverage, fan interpretations, and labor strife itself, the backlash was extensive. The NBA lockout, at one level, was about an increasing level of fan animus directed toward the league's primarily black players, much of which re-flected the insertion of race into the discussion. At another level, the 1998 lockout was about player divisions. Armen Keteyian, Harvey Araton and Martin Dardis in [their book] *Money Players*, describe the ways in which race, union divisions, and public perceptions impacted the 1998 lockout:

> As for the players, [player John] Salley said they had let the NBA and the agents divide them into warring factions the public perceived as the haves against the have nots. They came off looking, he said, like 'house Negroes and field Negroes.'
>
> Salley knew enough American history to understand this wasn't the first time something like this had occurred.
>
> 'Blacks in this country have always been divided and it never did us any good,' he said. 'The NBA is a very black league, so we must be careful of the message we send.'
>
> In effect, Salley's message was that no matter how successful it became, how big it got, 1970s racial perceptions would never go away for a predominantly black league selling to a white corporate crowd.
>
> Sadly, he may have been right, judging by the media's gen-eral response to the summer of labor strife. After at least ac-

knowledging baseball and hockey players had the right to fight for their best deal, many sports journalists more or less rolled their eyes and advised the basketball players to be happy with whatever they got. [NBA Commissioner David] Stern was held up as the sport's shining knight. [Player Michael] Jordan, as if he needed the money, was cast as a greedy infidel. One national sports commentator referred on television to Jordan's involvement as the 'equivalent of a drive-by shooting.'

That even brought out the less polished, 1960s liberal in Stern.

'F--- the people who say that Michael was being greedy, that he should just shut up and play,' Stern said. 'That's just code.'

## Demanding Silence from Players

In an effort to avoid the public divisions and to avoid the blowback from a media ready to pounce on any NBA player who inserts race or merely expresses a critical perspective, it seems the players and the union have gone to great lengths to disarm a previous source of leverage for the owners. This is most certainly evident in the relative silence from the players themselves (minus Derek Fisher who most certainly cannot be depicted as a hip-hop baller and part of the culture of extravagance, both of which are common narratives attached to the NBA's black players). It is also evident in the rhetoric seen from players when talking about playing overseas. It is never about the money but instead the love of the game; likewise, the efforts to highlight player participation in summer leagues where the love of the game is on full display, works to undercut the stereotype of the greedy black NBA player that was so prominent to the 1998 NBA lockout.

Carmelo Anthony wasn't calling players for a lack of courage but rather commenting on the cultural politics of the NBA and the ways in which both the league and its fans demand silence from its players, a fact that reflects new racism at worse. Be visible, play, and even make money but don't dare speak about injustices, inequalities, or the conditions of labor. In other words, "shut up and play."

# 7

# Fans Are the Real Victims of Sports Labor Strife

*Sally Jenkins*

*Sally Jenkins is a sports columnist for* The Washington Post *and the author of such books as* The Real All Americans: The Team That Changed a Game, a People, a Nation.

*Professional sports leagues take in massive revenues, and recent labor strife in professional sports is, in fact, caused by reckless spending. Someone has to pay the bills, and that inevitably means the fans, who have no voice in the negotiations. The only way for fans to ensure that the most popular leagues—particularly the NFL and the NBA—take their interest into consideration is to start spending their money not on football or basketball tickets but rather on sports that clearly appreciate their fans, such as soccer, tennis, and golf.*

When last we checked on the NFL labor negotiations, Commissioner Roger Goodell said, "We're going to continue to work hard at it." Then they broke for a four-day weekend. This is what passes for work in the NFL, which is only a seasonal job to begin with? When last we saw the NBA players, about 50 of them attended a negotiating session wearing solidarity T-shirts that read, "Stand." To which it was tempting to reply, "No, please, let it all fall down."

Maybe the current labor strife is actually healthy, if it helps us break our crack-like addiction to the major professional sports leagues. A common refrain from fans this spring is that we are helpless victims of the games we love to watch, caught in the middle of what are essentially internal arguments between owners and players over the margins of their wealth. But whose fault is it, exactly, if the pro leagues treat fans not as valued customers, but as knee jerk compulsives who will pay anything for a fix and endure any amount of abuse, and always come back for more?

## Out-of-Control Spending

We're now 104 days into the NFL lockout, and both sides are patting themselves on the back for finally negotiating for two or three days a week instead of pursuing mutually assured destruction for seven days a week. Meanwhile, the NBA is about to plunge into its own work stoppage if an agreement isn't reached by Thursday, despite the fact that the league is on a popular upswing: The Dallas-Miami finals were the second-most watched since 2004. In both cases, owners and players alike remain seemingly insensible to a central fact: The revenue they're fighting over is actually *other people's money*.

> *The leagues do not care about the average fan.*

Make no mistake about the true nature of these labor disagreements: They aren't classic employer-worker arguments. They are disputes between oligarchs and independent contractors, and they aren't so much about fair compensation as they are about how to shift the responsibility for out-of-control spending to someone else. Somehow, despite $4 billion in revenue, 22 of 30 NBA teams supposedly lost money last season. Somehow, despite $9 billion in revenue, and massive tax breaks and public assistance, NFL owners claim to be in a fiscal crisis. The reason for this is simple: reckless spending, huge gambles on new stadiums, and stupidly rich player contracts awarded by owners whose egos override their good sense.

Eventually, there will be compromise and concessions and everyone will return to work. There is one party, however, who won't be receiving any concessions: the ticket buyer.

Here is the fan cost index for the four major sports leagues, meaning the average cost for a family of four to attend a game. For the NFL it's $420.54, for the NBA it's $287.85, for Major League Baseball it's $197.36, and for the NHL it's $313.68.

Now consider another number: In 2009, the median household income in this country was $49,777.

## The Leagues Don't Care About Fans

This tells us something. What it tells us is that the leagues do not care about the average fan. They do not care about your condition, your preferences, your wishes, or your hardships. They care about mercilessly squeezing you, to offset their own profligacy, and they take it for granted that you will sacrifice the family vacation in order to help with the gas bills for their yachts. Eighteen NFL teams raised ticket prices, despite the lockout.

---

*The best way to push back against abusive practices and work stoppages is to punish leagues in the pocketbook.*

---

But the leagues may live to regret picking these fights, because in doing so they have called attention to their attitudes and practices, and provoked fans to ask some good questions. When taxpayers finance stadiums for private owners, shouldn't they get something in return, such as affordable seating, asks Brian Frederick of the Sports Fans Coalition, a lobbying group.

"I think more than anything they're just taking public support for granted," he says. "And the key to that has been their ability to orchestrate giant public subsidies to pay for their costs. The fact that they have a lot of their costs paid for enables them to bicker and fight over profit. The silver lining has been that it has exposed their business practices and given the public a glimpse of how much they've invested."

## Alternatives

The best way to push back against abusive practices and work stoppages is to punish leagues in the pocketbook. Do something else with the money—give it to a team that values its fans. Of the big four, baseball has done the best job of appreciating and remaining accessible to its constituency. On Saturday, you can see the [Washington] Nationals play for $2.

Or, you can buy four tickets to see [soccer team] D.C. United, and they will not only be delighted to have you, but actually give you some free stuff. A couple of beach towels, or, if you get the four-meal deal, you can get free hot dogs and sodas.

If you're really determined to spend a lot of money, why not buy tickets to the PGA [Professional Golfers' Association of America] Championship at Atlanta Athletic Club? Instead of spending $285 on a single game, you get seven days worth of passes to the tournament, plus free shuttles. If that's too much, then just spend $25 on a practice round.

If you don't like golf, then go to the Legg Mason Tennis Classic—where you can get a reserved seat for $20.

Or, if you're only into the major championships, take the train to New York and pay $60 for a grounds pass to first-week action of the U.S. Open [tennis tournament], and watch matches on 22 different courts.

Then there are the things you could do absolutely for free, things that are natural, and uncontrived. Hang on a fence and watch collegians play summer league baseball at your local park. Go to the Cape Hatteras lighthouse—a world class surfing spot—and watch, for not one cent, some of the most magical athletes on the face of the earth captured in the barrels of waves.

Come to think of it, maybe the NFL and the NBA unwittingly did us a favor with all of their haggling over profit margins. They invited us to imagine life without them. You know what? It would be pretty sweet. Maybe it would be less overwrought, and stressful, with better perspective. Turns out, there would be plenty to do—and a lot cheaper.

# 8

# Fans Will Always Return After a Sports Labor Dispute

*David J. Berri, Martin B. Schmidt, and Stacey L. Brook*

*David J. Berri, professor of economics at Southern Utah University, has published extensively on the economics of professional sports. Martin B. Schmidt is associate professor of economics at the College of William and Mary. Stacey L. Brook is associate professor of economics at the University of Sioux Falls.*

*Labor strife has little impact on fans' relationships with their teams. Sports writers and fan organizations typically warn that strikes or lockouts will result in a marked decline in fan support. However, statistical evidence shows that, in the seasons that follow a labor dispute, attendance returns to or exceeds pre-strike or pre-lockout levels.*

In 1964 Judge Robert Cannon, a lawyer representing the Major League Baseball Player Association (MLBPA), offered this insight into the plight of the American athlete. Testifying before the U.S. Senate, Cannon observed: "If I might, Senator, preface my remarks by repeating the words of Gene Woodling . . . 'we have it so good we don't know what to ask for next.' I think this sums up the thinking of the average major league ballplayer today."

The person who replaced Cannon at the MLBPA was the legendary Marvin Miller. Miller and his ultimate successor,

Donald Fehr, were able to find a few issues for players to quibble about with owners. For the most part such quibbling has been about how much of the revenue baseball creates each year should go to the players on the field and how much should go to the owners in the stands. . . . We would note that such animosity is not restricted to baseball. Labor disputes have also occurred in basketball, football, and hockey.

These fights are not just between players and owners, but also often involve the fans. . . . From 1981 to 2005 there have been seven disputes in these sports that have led to the cancellation of regular season games. Whether these disputes were officially a player strike or an ownership lockout fans have been forced to miss games because the players didn't come to play.

Since 1981 the league has averaged a major labor dispute, defined as a dispute that caused games to be cancelled, once every three or four years. The latest event [as of 2006], in the NHL, cancelled the 2004–05 season. This event in hockey allows the NHL to match both MLB and the NFL in the number of labor disputes that have resulted in cancelled games since 1981. All three leagues now have had two such events. So far the NBA is lagging behind. The 1998–99 lockout in basketball remains the only time the NBA has lost games to a labor dispute. In the summer of 2005 the NBA reached an agreement with its players well in advance of the 2005–06 season. The NBA's ability to reach an agreement without placing any games in serious jeopardy, though, has proven to be the exception to the general rule.

---

*Shouldn't the fans have a place at the negotiating table?*

---

To put the frequency of these tragedies in perspective, let's briefly consider how often work stoppages occur in the United States. The United States Department of Labor tells us that between 15 and 16 million workers in the United States belong to unions. There are approximately 4,000 unionized athletes in MLB, the NFL, the NBA, and the NHL. From 1981 these workers were involved in seven labor disputes. So if 4,000 workers are involved in seven stoppages, how many work stoppages should we see if we look at 16 million workers?

We know, who likes word problems? Here is the quick answer. If non-athletes experienced the same number of work stoppages as we see in sports, there would have been approximately 28,000 stoppages from 1981 to 2004. From 1981 to 2004 the same Department of Labor reports only 1,109 work stoppages in non-sports industries. In sum, these numbers tell us that athletes are about 25 times more likely to stop work when compared to workers in other industries in the United States.

Why are athletes so often involved in labor disputes with management? As we noted, these work stoppages occur because the players and owners cannot decide how to divide the billions of dollars in revenue sports generate each year. Given the small number of people involved, the dollars per person are quite substantial. Consider the 1994–95 labor strike in Major League Baseball. The strike led to the cancellation of the 1994 World Series and reduced the regular season in both 1994 and 1995. Roger Noll, an economist at Stanford, explained why the strike was so difficult to resolve. According to Noll, the owners' efforts to limit the growth in player salaries would have cost the players $1.5 billion over the life of the proposed agreement. The strike only cost the players $300 million. Given these numbers, it is easy to see why the players didn't come out and play.

Once we see the dollars involved, it is easier to understand why these disputes occur with such frequency. Still, there is one party that seems ignored at the negotiating table. As the media often notes, isn't it the fan who gives sports the billions of dollars the players and owners squabble about? Shouldn't the fans have a place at the negotiating table?

## The Summer of 2002

These were the questions people were asking during the summer of 2002. At this time negotiations between baseball players and owners were not progressing to the satisfaction of the MLBPA. Consequently, the players set a strike date of August 30. A strike by players would be the third such event in a little over twenty years.

The reaction of both the media and the fans could hardly be described as enthusiastic. A quick review of newspaper articles from August 2002 highlights the displeasure fans and the media had with those managing and playing the game of baseball. Specifically the fans, the media, and even the players and owners argued that if the game was taken away from the fans again, the fans would retaliate in the future. For many, the future of the game itself was in doubt. . . .

From the fans, the media, and the players we see a common theme. If the players walk we can expect the fans to walk.

In the summer of 2002 with the conventional wisdom being shouted from the mountaintops, two lone voices were speaking in the wilderness. On the pages of the *Los Angeles Times*, the *Cincinnati Inquirer*, the *Chicago Sun-Times*, the *Orlando Sentinel*, and the *San Jose Mercury News* two economists were quoted as saying the conventional wisdom was incorrect. According to these professors, although the fans frequently argue that they will walk, in the end it is all just talk. The two economists were named [David] Berri and [Martin] Schmidt, and the comments we made that summer were based upon research we had published in academic journals. Unfortunately, few people read academic journals. That's why we felt the need to write this book.

## Can the Fans Walk?

Let's begin with a confession. When we began this research we believed the conventional wisdom. It certainly seemed reasonable to us that fans would become unhappy with sports when the squabbling over money forces fans to find other entertainment options. Given this viewpoint, our purpose in looking at the impact labor disputes have on attendance was not to establish whether there was an impact. Of course there had to be an impact. We only wished to know how long it took fans to return to the game once the players came back. How big a penalty did the fans impose on players and owners when the games were taken away?

The methodology we followed came from the field of macroeconomics, a field where Schmidt has published extensively. To understand our approach to the study of strikes and attendance, we need to discuss, ever so briefly, a particular event in macroeconomic history. Let's return to the 1970s, a time when disco was king and polyester was the fabric of choice. At this time the price of oil rose dramatically. The sudden increase in the price of oil, coupled with the sight of millions of Americans dressed in polyester—okay, we made that part up—led to a decline in the growth rate of the U.S. economy. Eventually the economy recovered from the impact of higher oil prices. What researchers in macroeconomics wondered was how long it took the economy to recover from the external shock of rising oil prices.

Initially, we thought a player strike or ownership lockout had the same impact on fan attendance as higher oil prices have on economic growth. In a year where a strike happens, average fan attendance declines. Over time, though, fan attendance eventually returns. What we wished to measure was the time it took fans to return.

To answer this question we collected data on attendance for the NBA, NHL, NFL, and Major League Baseball. We then calculated how long it took fans of each league to return when labor disputes took away the games the fans love. . . .

## The Story in the NBA

The NBA has historically had relative labor peace. Up until the lockout of 1998 the NBA had prided itself on being the only major team sport in North America that had not lost games to a labor dispute. Why did the peace end? Well, the whole story would take us far from the subject of this chapter. For the most part the problem was typical: How should the revenue the NBA generates be divided between players and owners? Players themselves added a new wrinkle to the story when they argued about how to divide money between the stars and the non-stars the league employs. . . .

How did the lockout impact the fans' interest in this sport?

---

*NBA fans did not walk, in a statistical sense, when the players walked.*

---

In 1997–98 average attendance stood at 701,799 fans per team. The lockout of 1998–99 reduced the schedule by 32 games, and as a result aggregate attendance dropped to an average of 418,445; a total quite similar to what the league achieved over 82 games in 1982–83. In 1999–2000 the NBA returned to a full schedule and average attendance rose to 691,674. So the lockout cost the league about 10,000 fans per team, right?

Actually, this wouldn't be correct. We really can't be sure that drop in 10,000 fans was due to the lockout, or just part of the typical pattern we observe in league attendance. Although attendance generally rises, declines do occasionally happen. In 1990–91 NBA attendance declined 18,000 fans from the previous season. For the 1996–97 season we observe a decline of more than 7,000. Hence, a drop of 10,000 fans is not unusual. Can we argue the observed decline in 1999–2000 was significant in a statistical sense?

To answer this question we have to do more than just stare at the numbers. We need to measure how labor disputes impact attendance. Our specific method is called intervention analysis. Basically, intervention analysis looks at how the average value in a series of numbers changes given a specific intervention. If we study the macroeconomy, an intervention might be a sudden increase in oil prices. In our study of attendance, the intervention is a labor dispute that leads to the cancellation of games. . . .

When we employ intervention analysis to assess the impact of the NBA lockout on attendance we find that there wasn't any statistical impact. NBA fans did not walk, in a statistical sense, when the players walked.

## The Story in the Other "National" Sports

So maybe basketball fans didn't get the memo that labor disputes should cause fans to walk away. What about the National Hockey League and National Football League? Surely fans in these sports pay enough attention to care when games are taken away. . . .

Attendance in the 1960s was quite volatile, but the NHL did experience substantial growth beginning in the late 1970s. For the 1978–79 season average regular season attendance was 456,356. By 2003–04 attendance per team was 677,872. Over that 26-year period there is one substantial drop. This occurred in 1994–95 when a labor dispute in the NHL caused the schedule to be reduced from 84 games to only 48. As a result, attendance dropped from nearly 620,000 in 1993–94 to less than 360,000 in 1994–95. In 1995–96, though, despite playing a regular season that was only 82 games, the NHL actually saw attendance rise to more than 650,000 fans per team.

So after the lockout, attendance actually increased. On a per-game basis, the average NHL team after the lockout season drew more than 1,000 additional fans. Not surprisingly, intervention analysis fails to find a negative consequence from the lockout. NHL fans did not seem to respond in quite the way sportswriters predicted. We would add that the early returns from the 2005–06 season show that history for hockey fans does repeat itself. As of January 1, 2006, per-game attendance for the 2005–06 campaign, relative to the season before the 2004–05 lockout, had actually increased.

---

*In the end, the labor disputes do not seem to matter.*

---

Of course we are talking about hockey fans. Would we see the same if we look at the NFL? In 1982 a player strike cost the NFL seven regular season games. In 1987, another strike ultimately cost the NFL one regular season contest. With two strikes over such a short period of time, fans should have been enraged. . . .

Was there any permanent impact from either event? In 1981 the average NFL team attracted 485,964 fans in a season. In 1983 this number was reduced to 474,187, for a decline of nearly 12,000 fans. In 1986, the year before the next strike, attendance was 485,305 fans. In 1988 attendance declined less than 2,000 fans from the 1986 total. So in absolute terms, both strikes were followed by a decline in attendance. Was the decline statistically significant? Our intervention analysis indicates that neither event had a statistically significant impact on fan attendance.

So we have looked at four events and the story is the same each time. Players have gone on strike. Owners have locked out the players. In the end, the labor disputes do not seem to matter. Fans of basketball, hockey, and football still come back when the players return. . . .

## The Story in Our National Pastime

Although fans of the other sports may not care, those who follow our national pastime were clearly angry when baseball players threatened to go on strike. . . .

In contrast to the obvious pattern for all other work stoppages, the 1994–95 [MLB] labor dispute appears to have had an impact on attendance. In 1993 the average team attracted 2.51 million fans. The next complete season was 1996. For that season average attendance was only 2.15 million. In fact, the 2.51 million peak in 1993 is a record that still stands as we write in 2005. Clearly the evidence suggests that the strike of 1994–95 mattered. . . .

Actually, there is reason to believe that the 1993 increase was not likely to be permanent. Let us begin with the Colorado Rockies and Florida Marlins, the two expansion teams from that season. These two teams attracted nearly 7.5 million fans, a total that accounted for more than half of the observed increase in baseball attendance. The Rockies, playing in Mile High Stadium—home of the Denver Broncos [football team]—set a major league attendance record in their debut year with more than 4.4 million fans. Was the expansion effect permanent? The answer appears to be no. While the Colorado Rockies became the youngest expansion team to make the playoffs in 1995 and the Florida Marlins became the youngest expansion team to win the World Series in 1997, neither team has come within 600,000 of their 1993 levels. It would seem more likely that the record levels had more to do with the novelty of the new teams and with the Rockies playing in a stadium best suited for football.

The impact of football stadiums was not restricted to the Rockies. The top teams in baseball in 1993, Atlanta, Philadelphia, San Francisco, and Toronto, all shared a stadium with a football team. Toronto by itself topped four million fans in 1993. In essence, 1993 was a perfect storm, in a positive sense, for Major League Baseball attendance: two expansion teams opened in markets starved for baseball along with the best teams playing in very large stadiums.

By 1996 the perfect storm seems to have passed. Attendance in 1996 was 2.15 million. As our intervention analysis indicates, this is similar to what we observe for 1992. Again, 1992 was a very good year in the history of baseball attendance. If you wanted to argue that the 1994–95 strike devastated the game, you would have to argue that baseball was struggling in 1992 when attendance was quite near baseball's all-time high.

---

*Without resorting to legal action, the threat to walk is the only recourse for fans who wish to continue the flow of games they have grown to know and love.*

---

To hammer home this point, consider one last piece of evidence. Population since 1980 in the United States and Canada has grown approximately 30%. In this same time period, average attendance for Major League Baseball teams grew from 1.65 million in 1980 to 2.43 million in 2004. A bit of quick math reveals that this represents a 47% increase. Despite repeated labor disputes people are coming out to the ballpark in much greater numbers. Given these numbers it is hard to believe the conventional wisdom that the repeated fights between owners and players dramatically harm professional sports....

## A Few Lingering Questions

*Why do the media tell us that labor disputes threaten the survival of sports in America?* We cannot provide a definitive answer, but we can offer a bit of speculation. We would imagine that people choose to write about sports because they are interested in sports. A person who is interested in sports wants to talk about the games and personalities that make sports so fun. When a strike or lockout occurs these games are taken away. To make matters worse, sports writers are then asked to cover the labor dispute. So not only are sports writers not able to talk about the games they love, now they have to talk about the business of sports. When this happens, a person who loves sports must be quite unhappy. From the perspective of these writers, these labor disputes are clearly a tragedy. Labor disputes force writers to stop talking about what they love and start talking about salary caps and revenue sharing, which must be topics that leave much to be desired. . . .

*Why do fans tell us that they will not return when strikes and lockouts occur?* We must remember that we are academics. With that in mind, let's get all academic for a moment. We have seen that millions of fans attend sporting events each year. As economists, we generally argue that people take actions when the perceived benefits exceed the perceived costs. Given this basic axiom, we would argue that fans attend games because the benefits the fans get from attending the game exceed the costs in money and time spent. If this were not the case, people would just stay home. So, as economists, we would say that attending a game provides positive net benefits.

Now when labor disputes occur, all these future net benefits are threatened. In other words, we suspect that when these games are taken away, people who were going to attend these games are now worse off. How can fans prevent this loss of happiness? When the fans tell the players and owners that they will not return after a strike or lockout, these fans are now threatening the future benefits players and owners derive from sports. In other words, the threat to stay home threatens the wages and profits players and owners plan to earn in the future. Without resorting to legal action, the threat to walk is the only recourse for fans who wish to continue the flow of games they have grown to know and love.

Okay, so the fans are making a threat. Is this threat credible? Well, actually it's not. The fans are basically saying that if the players and owners do not settle today, in the future fans will forgo the pleasure they derive from sports. Fans are really saying, "if you don't do as I wish today, I will hurt myself tomorrow." This is very much like a child who doesn't get his way promising to hold his breath until he turns blue. Given the obvious love many fans have for sports, the promise of retribution tomorrow can't be believed.

# 9

# The Success of the NFL Proves Collective Bargaining Benefits Everyone

*David Madland and Nick Bunker*

*David Madland is director of the American Worker Project at the Center for American Progress, a liberal think tank. Nick Bunker is a research assistant with the Economic Policy team at the center.*

*Labor negotiations in the NFL have benefited players and owners alike, as both player salaries and overall team values have risen significantly since the last collective bargaining agreement in 2006. This mutual success proves that leagues with a strong union to represent players and a well-organized league office to represent the owners fare much better than those without, such as American baseball and European soccer leagues, where only a few wealthy teams prosper. Furthermore, the prosperity of the NFL suggests that societies in which the needs of both workers and owners are addressed will experience similar gains.*

The opening of the NFL season, usually an exciting time for fans, players, and owners, may be bittersweet this year because the owners of the National Football League are threatening to lock out the players next season—meaning canceled games—if the owners and the players' union cannot agree to a new collective bargaining agreement by March 2011.

David Madland and Nick Bunker, "The NFL's Win-Win Labor Agreement," The Center for American Progress Action Fund, September 8, 2010. http://www .americanprogressaction.org. Copyright © 2010 by The Center for American Progress. All rights reserved. Reproduced by permission.

These negotiations are important not just to NFL fans but to all Americans because they show that collective bargaining—the process where unionized workers and management negotiate wages, benefits, and working conditions—can create significant benefits for both workers and owners. This is a process that most Americans no longer have first-hand knowledge of. The reason: Just 7 percent of the private-sector workforce today is unionized. That's why the latest round of negotiations can help illustrate how unions can help level the playing field between workers and management.

## A Win-Win Labor Accord

Both NFL players and owners have done quite well under the current collective bargaining agreement. Median player salaries rose 9.4 percent between 2006 and 2009, and team values rose an impressive 16.2 percent over the same period. Such a win-win labor accord is obviously something both sides should want to renew.

---

*A look at the data that is available clearly shows that the current labor agreement ... is a great success not only for the players but for the owners as well.*

---

That's not the case today in many other industries, where some corporate managers view the current economic downturn as an opportunity to seek concessions from workers and cut costs, with even some quite profitable companies demanding that workers do the same job for far less than they once made. So when Drew Brees, the quarterback of the world champion New Orleans Saints, and other NFL stars negotiate together to seek the best deal they can get, ordinary workers who may be good at their job, but perhaps not the best in the world may recognize the importance of joining together to ensure they are treated fairly.

The owners argue that the current collective bargaining agreement signed in 2006 did not serve them well—despite the rising value of their franchises—and that the cost of building new stadiums and the upkeep of league-owned assets are eating into their bottom line. These specific claims are hard to evaluate because only the publicly owned Green Bay Packers release any detailed financial information—details that show the team is quite profitable, though somewhat less so during the Great Recession. The NFL hasn't released data on any other teams, including those likely to be much more profitable, such as the Dallas Cowboys and Washington Redskins.

## The Success of the Current Agreement

But a look at the data that is available clearly shows that the current labor agreement, an extension of the original collective bargaining agreement signed in 1993, is a great success not only for the players but for the owners as well. The league, by combining a strong union with strong league institutions, created an effective model that delivers financial success across the board—an accomplishment that other leagues have not replicated, as a comparison with Major League Baseball and several international soccer teams clearly shows. NFL players' salaries and the value of NFL teams grew smartly over this time period, even during the recession.

The signing of the 1993 collective bargaining agreement brought the advent of the salary cap, free agency, and more than 15 years of labor peace in the NFL. It also created a system that has fostered prosperity for both the owners and the players. Player salaries are kept in line with revenue by the salary cap, and revenue sharing ensures that all NFL franchises share in the success of the league. As structured under the current collective bargaining agreement, the salary cap is set as a percentage of total revenue, the league's revenue less a deduction for owners. The 2006 agreement set that percentage at 57.5 percent for the 2009 season, as detailed on page 96 of the contract.

Players have done quite well under these terms, with the median NFL salary in 2009 equaling $790,000 a year, according to data provided by the National Football League Players Association. Since 2000, the earliest year with data available, we calculate that the median NFL player salary increased by 79 percent, and since signing the 2006 extension, median player salary has increased by 9.4 percent, meaning that player salaries have increased even during very tough recession years.

Similarly, the owners have done quite well under the current agreement, despite their claims to the contrary. Since 1999, the year *Forbes* magazine started to value NFL franchises, the average franchise value has risen by 171 percent, so that by 2009, the average franchise was worth $1.04 billion—with 19 of the 32 franchises valued over $1 billion—according to *Forbes*'s annual "Business of Football" valuations. Since 2006 when the current CBA [collective bargaining agreement] was signed, the average NFL franchise value has increased by 16.2 percent, a growth rate that is faster than the median player salary increase. As a result, it appears that NFL owners are doing fine, but if the league's financials reflect a different reality, then the owners should release these numbers.

## Owners Have Especially Benefited

And compared to other professional sports leagues, the NFL collective bargaining agreement looks like it served the owners especially well. Baseball may be America's pastime, but Major League Baseball can't stack up financially against the National Football league. Likewise, soccer has a worldwide appeal unmatched by any other sport, as evidenced by the enthusiasm surrounding the World Cup this past summer. Yet the financial value of European soccer leagues can't rival that of the National Football League.

Specifically, in 2010 the average value of a Major League Baseball franchise was $491 million, approximately half of that of the average NFL team. Not only are baseball franchises worth less on average, but the variation in value is quite large. In 2010, the New York Yankees were valued at $1.6 billion, equivalent to the value of the top NFL teams. But the Pittsburgh Pirates, the least valuable baseball franchise, was valued at $289 million. In contrast, the least valuable NFL franchise, the Jacksonville Jaguars, was valued at $725 million.

---

*This inequality in international soccer is the result of both weak unions and weak league institutions.*

---

In addition, since 2001, the earliest year data is available, the value of the average MLB team only grew by 7.3 percent per year on average, while NFL franchises grew by an average of 12 percent. The MLB Players Association has a history of success in advocating for its players, but the league lacks many of the redistribution mechanisms of the NFL, including a salary cap, league-negotiated television deals, and a strong revenue sharing system. The strong union, strong top-team, weak-league model has served MLB players and some owners well though the league itself has certainly not prospered as much as the NFL.

Similarly, the soccer clubs of England, Spain, and Italy attract the world's best players from across the globe, and clubs such as Manchester United and Inter Milan can claim fans on several continents. Yet the average value of the top 20 most valuable soccer clubs in all the leagues of Europe was $632 million in 2010, according to *Forbes*, meaning the average NFL team was worth considerably more than the average of the top clubs from the English, Spanish, Italian, German, and French leagues.

# Inequality in International Soccer

The variation in value of top soccer teams is quite wide. Manchester United, the English powerhouse, was valued at $1.8 billion in 2010, the wealthiest team on *Forbes's* World's Most Valuable Sports Teams list, just edging out the Dallas Cowboys. Rangers F.C. of the Scottish Premier League is worth $194 million, according to *Forbes*. This disparity would be amazing if the clubs were in the same league, but amazingly Rangers was the 20th most valuable soccer club in all of Europe in 2009. Everton, which competes with Manchester United in the English Premier League, was valued at $207 million but is far from a cellar dweller in the league. If data were available, the variation in wealth within domestic European leagues would be incredible. It is important to note that these figures are for the top 20 clubs in all of Europe and could be considerably different if we knew the financial status of other clubs.

This inequality in international soccer is the result of both weak unions and weak league institutions. Players' associations are much weaker and there are no collective bargaining agreements in the English Premier League, the most lucrative league. Television deals are not split equally, but divided out according to performance. Furthermore, the teams at the bottom of the standings are demoted from the top league and replaced by other teams in a system known as regulation and promotion. This weak-union, strong-team, weak-league model results in wildly unequal leagues where only a few teams make substantial amounts of money.

Through collective bargaining agreements and strong league institutions, the NFL boasts a system that creates wealth for all of its owners and players. The institutional models of Major League Baseball and European soccer leagues do not produce anything rivaling the broad-based prosperity the NFL creates. As the NFL owners and the NFLPA [National Football League Players Association] representatives continue their negotiations, they should look at other sports leagues and re-member how well the current system has served them.

# 10

# NFL Labor Dispute Reflects Wider Rift Between Workers and Employers

*Michael Schottey*

*Michael Schottey is a columnist and associate editor at the Bleacher Report, a sports news website.*

*The conflict between labor and management in the NFL is a microcosm of the growing unrest between employees and employers in the United States. Just as in Wisconsin, where conservative governor Scott Walker attempted in 2011 to slash the pay and benefits of public employees by eliminating their right to negotiate collectively and implementing budget cuts by mandate, NFL owners want the players to accept a reduction in pay without negotiations based on the current financial situation of the league. In both cases, the employees are labeled greedy while the employers refuse to negotiate fairly.*

As labor issues heat up between the NFL and the NFL Players Association, everyone seems to have their own opinion on which side is right and which side is more greedy or entitled. Not surprisingly, many of those same battle lines are heating up [in early 2011] over events in Madison, Wisconsin.

## "Us vs. Them" Is All Relative

One of the biggest misnomers of the NFL labor issue is that it is just "millionaires fighting with billionaires." Everyone says it, but that statement just isn't true. The vast majority of the members in the NFLPA aren't signing Peyton Manning-like deals or traveling via private jets.

Most NFL players only play two or three years in the league, they play at the end of the roster or on practice squads and are constantly looking for other jobs because they could be cut at any moment.

---

*This labor battle is like every labor battle before it. It is about employers vs. employees.*

---

For every Tom Brady, there are 10 Keith Fitzhughs.

Fitzhugh, a one-time Mississippi State football standout, always dreamed about playing in the NFL, but chose railroad conducting over the New York Jets because the former offered better pay and more stability.

In the end, the amount of money the players make, or that the owners are worth is a complete red herring to the discussion.

This labor battle is like every labor battle before it. It is about employers vs. employees. It doesn't matter how rich either side is. The success of the business depends on both, and the wealth of both is relative to the success of the business.

A stark contrast to the immensely successful NFL, is the bankrupt state of Wisconsin.

Wisconsin state employees, by all accounts, live comfortably, working hard for their money in mostly-thankless jobs that are necessary for society to run smoothly. They work with slashed budgets and diminishing staffs. They work while those around them are laid off, wondering if they are next.

The business that is the state of Wisconsin is failing, and its employees are feeling the pinch.

The current economic climate of the country pities neither of these groups and envies both. With unemployment rates falling from all-time highs, many Americans dream of state employee salaries and wouldn't know what to do with NFL practice squad pay.

In the NFL, and in Wisconsin, no one would argue that plenty of people would love to be paid so well, or at all. However, too many on the outside are comparing apples to oranges and not looking at the actual matters at hand.

---

*The worst thing for the NFL and for the state of Wisconsin would be a work stoppage.*

---

## It's Not Always About Money

In the media, and around water coolers, everyone wants to talk about money.

Throwing out dollar amounts and screaming about entitlement is ubiquitous in discussions of both the NFL labor negotiations and Wisconsin politics. On the other hand, listening to Wisconsin state employees or NFL players, those two groups aren't concerned about dollars as much as they are about common sense.

George Atallah, Assistant to the Executive Director of the NFLPA, states, "Players just want a fair deal."

Over and over, the union has expressed willingness to make concessions for the good of the game.

They just don't want to make concessions for the good of the owners' bottom line.

In Wisconsin, state employees obviously don't want to hamstring the government into bankruptcy. If the state goes under, they wouldn't have slashed wages, they'd have none. In fact, state employees recently made 100 million dollars worth of concessions to aid the state budget. They've also expressed willingness to negotiate further cuts.

The problem is, NFL owners and Wisconsin governor Scott Walker don't want to negotiate—at least, not fairly.

NFL owners want players to accept a deal without having to disclose their own financial records. The NFL has never been more successful, popular, or lucrative, but owners want the players to trust that teams are hemorrhaging money.

Scott Walker wants to take away the union's right to negotiate by legislating a solution. Rather than come to the table together, Walker wants to fundamentally change the way state employees unions across the nation operate.

In both situations, negotiations will settle matters, but all sides have to be willing to sit down.

## "Take It or Leave It" Just Won't Fly

The worst thing for the NFL and for the state of Wisconsin would be a work stoppage.

In the NFL, it would be a lockout—owners shutting the doors and telling players to stay home until a compromise is reached. In Wisconsin, a strike is looming as teachers have already taken sick days to protest the law on the legislative floor.

The final similarity between these two situations is how much people espouse the empty platitude of "take it or leave it."

NFL fans are really good at telling NFL players to "find a real job" if they don't like their multi-million dollar salary.

(*Nota Bene* [take note]: Being a professional athlete is a real job, and one of the most hazardous ones at that.)

Now, a similar strain is picking up decibels in the heartland as teachers and other public employees are being told to "take the deal or find another job."

The problem is, that isn't how unions work.

Unions bargain collectively. If the NFL Players decide to "leave it." The NFL will cease to exist. Unless, of course, fans want to watch [team owners] Stephen Ross and William Ford play catch each Sunday.

If the Wisconsin state employees decide to "leave it" and find other jobs, the state of Wisconsin shuts down. Scott Walker and the state legislature can't teach every child and clean every bathroom.

The thing people have to remember—fans, media and both sides in these two arguments—is that negotiation is the key to success.

In the NFL, both sides have to be willing to sit down and work together. Neither side can impose anything on the other, because that isn't how negotiations work.

---

*Neither of these situations will be solved without negotiation and compromise.*

---

In Wisconsin, matters will be solved by working together, not against each other.

## Two Vastly Different Situations, Eerie Similarities

The differences between a classroom and a NFL playing field are immense.

These two hot-button topics in the news today—one in politics, the other in sports—are eerily similar. They are similar because they are so often discussed in ways that don't accurately portray the actual issues.

Neither of these situations are about rich people versus richer people. Neither of these situations are about the entitlement of the workers verses those in America without jobs. Neither of these situations is solely about money. Neither of these situations will be solved without negotiation and compromise.

If those outside the discussion are willing to see the situations for what they're really about, perhaps those inside the discussion will be that much more willing to move past rhetoric and find a solution.

# 11

# Players' Unions Encourage Perpetual Labor Strife

*Richard A. Epstein*

*Richard A. Epstein is professor emeritus of law at the University of Chicago Law School. His books include* Design for Liberty: Private Property, Public Administration, and the Rule of Law; The Case Against the Employee Free Choice Act; *and* Supreme Neglect: How to Revive Constitutional Protection for Private Property.

*Professional sports leagues in America are monopolies that are only allowed to operate because they are granted an antitrust exemption by the federal government, one that is centered on the players' right to negotiate collectively. When the players do not get what they want in negotiations, as in the 2011 NFL lockout, they are free to dissolve or "decertify" their union and file antitrust lawsuits against the league, which forces owners to settle in order to avoid a long, expensive trial. By relying on decertification as a negotiating tactic, players' unions actively encourage labor strife and extended lockouts.*

NFL players want it both ways—to bargain under the best parts of labor and antitrust law.

In recent months [in 2011], most of the public attention on the union question has been devoted to the status of collective bargaining rights for public unions in such bellwether states as Wisconsin and Ohio. In those cases, the key issue is

Richard A. Epstein, "Stop the Football Merry-Go-Round," *Defining Ideas: A Hoover Institution Journal*, March 29, 2011. Copyright © 2011 by the Hoover Institution Press. All rights reserved. Reproduced by permission.

whether the outsized structure of pension and benefit programs can be pared back without a fundamental restructuring of the negotiating system that generated them in the first place.

At the same time, and at the opposite end of the financial spectrum, a second labor dispute is now in motion that could result in the cancellation of the National Football League's 2011–2012 season because of a breakdown in the renegotiation of the players' labor contracts. The looming disintegration of collective bargaining with public unions is not relevant to this particular debate, for there is surely enough to go around in one of the world's most lucrative sports. The question here, rather, has to do with the division of the spoils between management and players in a sport that has proved spectacularly popular in recent years. That issue in turn arises because of the peculiar structure of these negotiations, which pits management en masse against the labor unions in what appears to be yet another illustration of the fragility of collective bargaining arrangements in which each side has no option but to deal with its opponents.

---

*The NFLPA has skillfully exploited the imperfect intersection between the labor and the antitrust laws in order to gather for itself the best of both worlds.*

---

## Decertification of the Union

In most ordinary labor negotiations, everyone understands that labor unions gain real advantages under the National Labor Relations Act of 1935, which was crafted for their benefit. Yet on March 11, 2011, the National Football League Players Association [NFLPA] decertified itself in the wake of prolonged and fruitless negotiations with the team owners. Although the owners have protested that the players had bargained in bad faith under the labor statutes, the former union members claim that none of that matters now that the union itself has been decertified by the players.

The question is, why did the players take this weird legal stand? To anyone who is, as I surely was, ignorant of the NFL's checkered labor-relations history, the NFLPA's actions made as much sense as laying down a knife in a street fight. Yet unions—even players' unions—are not known for their tendency to commit financial suicide, and rest assured that the erstwhile union members did not do any such foolish thing.

On this matter, the class action complaint filed by the Patriots' Tom Brady—and other NFL luminaries in their individual capacities—dispels any budding illusions about self-destructive unions. The back-story here is that the NFLPA has skillfully exploited the imperfect intersection between the labor and the antitrust laws in order to gather for itself the best of both worlds.

## Leagues Need to Preserve Competitive Balance

To step back a moment, the key insight here is that competitive athletic leagues are not like typical competitive industries. In standard competitive markets dealing with the sale of, say, computers or shaving cream, each firm hopes to gain the largest possible share of the overall market, without showing any solicitude for the survival of its opponents. In competitive leagues, however, the road to financial perdition is paved with weekly blowouts of league patsies by well-heeled teams. "On any given Sunday," as they used to say in the NFL, any team in the league could beat any other. To ensure their own popularity and financial success, owners and players alike need to assure some measure of parity among teams to generate the nail biters that keep fans coming back. The objective in this business is not to crush your opponents. It is to be just better enough than your stalwart opponents in order to win championships. This model is truly ubiquitous, for it is the only one that works in league sports, no matter what the profit levels of the teams are.

If the NFL were treated as a single firm, organizing a draft, imposing salary caps, and requiring compensation for players who sign with other teams, these measures would only constitute the internal housekeeping that is intended to preserve the needed competitive balance of the league. These internal operations would take on no antitrust significance because they do not involve any contract or combination among rival firms. But since these teams have independent managers, shareholders, and brands, the courts have uniformly condemned these cooperative league actions as per se illegal "horizontal" restraints of trade entered into by these competitive businesses. The uncompromising dictates of the antitrust laws do not use a "rule of reason" for these horizontal arrangements, their huge economic benefits notwithstanding. Essentially the courts have chosen to attack the monopoly elements of unions, without making any allowances for their huge efficiency gains.

Enter modern labor law, which insulates all collective bargaining agreements from antitrust scrutiny. Under this umbrella, the NFLPA and the owners do two things. First, they adopt an efficient set of contract restrictions to ensure needed team parity. Second, they shed blood in deciding how to divide the $8.5 billion in NFL revenues.

In 2008, the owners opted out of a six-year agreement that had been extended in 2006. Thus, the contract ended after the 2010 season. Their reason for doing this was pure self-interest—to gain a bigger slice of the pie by renegotiation with the players union. In response, the NFLPA demanded ten years of audited financial statements to get a read of the teams' financial positions. But national labor law requires these disclosures only when management pleads poverty, not when it goes after more profits. It also allows the owners to lock out the players after a bargaining impasse.

## The Merry-Go-Round

This is where the players chose to get off (or is it on?) the merry-go-round. Under current law, once a union decertifies itself, the antitrust law once again brands that lockout an illegal collective refusal to deal. And so, the players begged for a return to the natural "competitive" state—which, if implemented, would ruin both sides financially, as explained earlier. In so doing, the players used a huge club of treble damage antitrust actions against the owners. The players also brought all sorts of state law claims, saying, for example, that teams remain obligated to uphold individual player contracts even if the season is canceled.

---

*Congress should today take the modest step of passing legislation that legalizes all the standard practices now embodied in the NFL labor agreements.*

---

To make matters worse, this entire wacky scheme is embedded for all time in a 1993 antitrust consent decree that contains an odd provision whereby, as the players allege, "the NFL insisted on the right to terminate the [settlement agreement] if the players did not reform a union within thirty days." Wow. The players eagerly complied, but in exchange the NFL agreed to waive its antitrust defenses after any future NFLPA decertification. And so the same cycle is preserved for the next labor dispute.

So here is the bottom line. The players get to choose whether and when they bargain under either the labor or the antitrust law. Their best strategy is to first denounce standard business practices under the antitrust law and then reinstate them under the labor law once peace returns. Holding all the cards, they keep a lion's share of the pie.

## Bar Players' Antitrust Advantage

Without a doubt, collective bargaining works badly with both public and private unions, as the Wisconsin saga [the conflict in 2011 between the state government and public unions] so clearly demonstrates. But if that system governs NFL labor relations, the players should be barred by statute from using the antitrust law to get their way, by hypocritically denouncing a set of antitrust violations that promptly become the heart of their next lucrative labor agreement.

To stop this charade, Congress should today take the modest step of passing legislation that legalizes all the standard practices now embodied in the NFL labor agreements, denying players the antitrust advantage through decertification. That recalibration leaves them no worse off than any other labor union that deals with a unitary employer.

Indeed, it can be argued that even that first step leaves players in far too strong a position. Players know that salaries could be slashed under the older "reserve clause" regime that forced them to negotiate within the league only with the team that signed them. But if salaries were lower, the league would also prove more stable, because no outsized salary demands from an individual star could shut the NFL down. Remember that baseball did not close its doors the years that Babe Ruth and Joe DiMaggio held out for more money.

That institutional stability has real positive external effects that both the present labor and antitrust laws ignore. Right now, the breakdown in negotiations works a real hardship on fans, hot dog vendors, groundskeepers, restaurants, newspapers, and broadcasters whose livelihood depends on having a season. And for what? The irony here is that the only thing that is worse socially than a monopoly among team owners is a bilateral monopoly in which team owners are forced to share their gains with the players. In today's intellectual climate, there's no chance whatsoever of going back to those good old days.

Nor is there, I might add, any chance of forcing a split up of the NFL's two conferences, the AFC and the NFC, which would lead to the best of all worlds: measures to assure parity within leagues, and competition between leagues. The players give up their unions in favor of a choice between teams in two leagues. The management gives up its solid front in favor of labor peace. The rest of us can still watch a Super Bowl at the end of the season, with a special antitrust exemption. It may be too much to ask in the current milieu, which prefers the use of what the late [economist] John Kenneth Galbraith used to call countervailing powers.

Short of this fanciful transformation, what should be done right now to harmonize the labor law and the antitrust law to stop the current football merry-go-round brought about by systematic decertification? Let the laws be reconfigured in ways that recognize that first-rate competition on the field requires managed competition at the negotiating table. At that point management and labor will be less likely to use old-fashioned methods to do each other in.

# 12

# Players' Unions Give Athletes a Voice That Non-Union Workers Don't Have

*Paul Frymer and Dorian T. Warren*

*Paul Frymer is an associate professor in the Department of Politics at Princeton University and the author of* Black and Blue: African Americans, the Labor Movement, and the Decline of the Democratic Party. *Dorian T. Warren is an assistant professor of International and Public Affairs at Columbia University.*

*Players' unions and the Occupy Wall Street movement are motivated by a similar concern over insider deals that have resulted in a massive transfer of wealth away from the working class into the hands of the already wealthy. On the national scale, such a transfer of wealth can be directly correlated to the decline in union membership among American workers. Likewise, professional athletes need a strong union to combat rules that allow owners to demand concessions from the players even in times of record profits.*

L eBron James is as far as you can get from the 99 percent.

The NBA superstar is paid more than $16 million a year as a forward for the Miami Heat and has a $90 million contract with Nike. After his team lost the NBA finals to Dallas in June, he told griping fans to go back to the humdrum reality of "the real world," while he retreated to his recently purchased $9 million home in South Beach.

So James may seem to share nothing with the 99 percent—in [the protest movement] Occupy Wall Street's terms, the vast majority of American workers, who suffer in a culture of unabashed greed that has created a historic gulf of inequality between the richest Americans and everyone else.

---

*[The union gives players] certain contractual rights such as job security, health and retirement benefits, and a significant voice in the way their company is run.*

---

## Players Are Beholden to Owners

But he and the other NBA players have something important in common with the 99 percent. James is an employee of the Miami Heat. Despite his recent tweet hinting that he will try to join the National Football League if the NBA lockout continues, he finds himself, like most Americans, beholden to the owners and managers who control his workplace and industry. If the owners want to lock out the workers, or leave the country in search of greater profits, he—like American workers whose jobs have disappeared overseas—is left with few options. He is beholden to team owners who are not always upfront about their revenue and profits, and who are claiming a right to make more money without equitably sharing it with the workers who make the huge windfalls possible.

In the split between NBA players and owners, the players are voicing frustrations that may seem awfully similar to what the Occupy Wall Street protesters are saying. The players are accusing the owners—who keep recording yearly profits as a group while claiming hardship and the need for belt-tightening—of playing by different rules; avoiding public scrutiny; and benefiting from a range of insider deals, bailouts and protections without sharing the profits.

At issue in this dispute is whether the league can impose a tighter salary cap on the teams, which would effectively lower the salaries of the players. The other major conflict is over how "basketball-related income"—which includes revenue from the sale of tickets, parking, food at concession stands, player jerseys and broadcast rights—will be split between players and owners. Until now, players got a slight majority of this revenue. This made sense, since it was superstars such as Michael Jordan and Magic Johnson, and now Kobe Bryant and LeBron James, who brought the league to new heights in popularity and profits. The owners, however, say it is unsustainable to maintain high salaries and existing profit margins. They want a 50-50 split of the basketball-related income.

The players have remained united and responded angrily to NBA Commissioner David Stern's initial threats of cancelling the season. Dwyane Wade, James's teammate and one of the league's biggest stars, yelled at the commissioner in a heated meeting, saying: "You're not pointing your finger at me. I'm not your child." Steve Nash, two-time NBA most valuable player, questioned the owners' representation of their finances, tweeting, "Why are the owners unwilling to negotiate in good faith?"

Despite some optimism Thursday, Stern late on Friday canceled all games through Nov. 30 [2011]. Going into the weekend, talks remained stalled around the issue of sharing basketball-related income.

## Most Americans Lack the Support of a Union

One of the reasons NBA players should ultimately resolve this conflict—and have greater influence than most workers in such a dispute—is that they are, unlike 88 percent of their fellow Americans, members of a labor union. This gives them certain contractual rights such as job security, health and retirement benefits, and a significant voice in the way their company is run.

The nation's historic rise in income inequality and insecurity has been matched by a decline in union membership. Half a century ago, roughly one in three American workers was a union member, whereas today union membership has dropped to just 7 percent in the private sector and less than 12 percent overall, the lowest in 70 years. For workers, this decline can mean the absence of job security or benefits, as well as falling wages. In 2010, union members made on average $10,000 a year more than non-union workers, and economists have shown that even the prospect of unionization has led to rising wages in different industries.

When you're at the mercy of an employer without a labor union to support you—the situation that nine out of 10 American workers face—inequality is guaranteed to rise. And it's this bleak reality that is fueling Occupy Wall Street anger.

---

*If [LeBron] James succeeds in his latest fight, he can bring his talents not just to South Beach, but to the 99 percent of Americans who could use his help.*

---

Elected officials have recently directed outrage about the economic collapse and rising inequality toward unions instead of Wall Street. That was one tactic that Wisconsin Gov. Scott Walker (R) used this year when he eliminated collective-bargaining rights for public-sector employees in his state.

NBA players are in a stronger position to make demands and extract victories from their employers than Wisconsin schoolteachers, because they are public figures in a highly specialized and valued industry. That's why the owners haven't just hired a set of replacement workers—a move that is increasingly typical of other industries in America.

## A Familiar Power Imbalance

No one can really call the 6'8", 250-pound James vulnerable or a worker without a voice. But his struggle does, in a key way, mirror the power imbalance that the average American employee confronts. Both face a culture that believes workers should have no voice in the everyday life of the workplace or the broader economy. When Wade asserts that he does not want to be treated like Stern's child, he is expressing what many Americans around the country feel—that those who work should have a greater say in working conditions, profits and economic growth.

All Americans, whether on the basketball court or the shop floor, ought to have a meaningful voice, bargaining power and some way to retain a sense of dignity in a bad economy. Hopefully, if James succeeds in his latest fight, he can bring his talents not just to South Beach, but to the 99 percent of Americans who could use his help.

# 13

# Adopting European System Would Eliminate Labor Issues in US Sports

*David Berri*

*David Berri is a professor of economics at Southern Utah University and coauthor of* The Wages of Wins: Taking Measure of the Many Myths in Modern Sport.

*Professional sports teams in the United States should adopt a European-style model to avoid the next major labor dispute. In European soccer, teams that play well are promoted to more lucrative leagues, while perennial losers are relegated to leagues of lower status. If they play poorly enough for long enough, a team may be eliminated from competition altogether. If this model was applied to American sports, there would be little reason to demand concessions from players and owners to support teams that fail to produce wins and the revenue that comes with them.*

Soon after presents are opened on Christmas morning, the NBA—after a lengthy lockout—will finally open its 2011–12 season with a slate of five games. Although NBA fans are pleased the lockout has ended, they'd probably prefer that it had never happened. Unfortunately for fans of pro sports in North America, such disputes frequently cause games to be missed. But maybe there is a free market solution to this problem to be found in, of all places, Europe.

David Berri, "A Free Market Solution (from Europe) to the Labor Problems in North American Sports," *Freakonomics* (blog), December 20, 2011. http://www.freakonomics.com. Copyright © 2011 by David Berri. All rights reserved. Reproduced by permission.

Although we tend to think such disputes are a contest between labor and management, frequently the real conflict—as noted in my recent posts here—is between small and large market teams. In North American sports, team revenue seems to depend on the size of the market where the team plays. For example, according to Forbes.com, the New York Knicks had $226 million in revenues in 2009–10, while the Milwaukee Bucks brought in just $92 million. A similar story is seen in baseball, where the New York Yankees brought in $427 million in 2010, while the Pittsburgh Pirates had only $160 million in revenues.

---

*North American sports leagues use central planners to determine the location of sports teams. In contrast, European sports leagues rely on the market.*

---

Such revenue disparities often cause small market teams to demand more money. Ideally—from the owners' perspective—this money comes from the players, which is what we saw happen in the NBA dispute, where the players just took a pay cut. In baseball, the players have historically been unwilling to accept wage cuts for small market teams. Consequently, baseball has transferred—via the luxury tax—money directly from large market teams to small market teams.

If we look to Europe, though, we might see a better approach. To understand it, let's consider the arguments of [economist] Frederich Hayek, who argued that a centrally planned economy can't work as well as a free market one because the central planner could never have enough information to make adequate decisions. OK, but what does this have to do with sports?

Essentially, North American sports leagues use central planners to determine the location of sports teams. In contrast, European sports leagues rely on the market.

## European Sports Leagues

For those unfamiliar with the nature of European sports leagues, let's briefly describe the promotion and relegation system. In a league such as the English Premier League, the bottom three teams in each season are demoted to the Championship League (a lesser league). The top three teams from the Championship League are then promoted to the Premier League. Consequently, losers in the Premier League—as we see in a capitalistic market—are punished financially. And success in the Championship League is clearly rewarded.

By allowing teams to play their way into the league, any market can have a team. Consider the allocation of teams in the English Premier League today. Currently there are five different teams in the London area. This makes sense, since London is by far the biggest urban area in England. Of course, New York is the largest metropolitan area in the United States, and in each of the major North American sports leagues there are no more than two teams located in the Big Apple (a point I will return to in a moment).

*Failure in North American sports is simply not allowed by the central planners.*

In the English Premier League, though, there is no restriction on where the teams can be located. So we see three teams in the Birmingham area (second largest urban area), but Leeds (third largest in population) and Bristol (fifth largest in population) have zero teams. And the two teams leading the Premier League thus far this season are in Manchester (fourth largest in population).

A central planner would probably never have placed two teams in Manchester while skipping over Leeds and Bristol.

In contrast, North American sports leagues are planned. For a market to acquire a team, the existing owners must first agree to expand—or move an existing team. And then any new ownership group must be approved by those very same owners.

## Failure Is Not Allowed

The existing owners have insisted that the large markets be restricted (again, New York doesn't have more than two teams in any of the major sports leagues). Consequently the league has moved into smaller markets. To make this work, the smaller markets are encouraged to assist the team via taxpayer subsidies for new arenas. Furthermore, if the team struggles, high draft picks and/or luxury tax dollars are transferred to the team in the name of creating parity.

All of this is done in an effort to ensure that all teams are profitable. Yes, failure in North American sports is simply not allowed by the central planners. Not surprisingly (and consistent with Hayek's contention that central planning doesn't work that well) chronic failures—like the L.A. Clippers and Pittsburgh Pirates—are not uncommon.

---

*In North American sports leagues, when incompetence leads to shortfalls in revenue, the league turns to the players and demands wage cuts to compensate the losers.*

---

Once upon a time, the Pirates often contended for and won titles. But since 1992, the Pirates have always been losers. Their ineptitude, however, pales in comparison to the Clippers. Since the Clippers came to California in 1978, the team has had only three winning seasons. And one of these was the first season in San Diego in 1978–79.

Had the Pirates and Clippers played in something like the English Premier League, the Pirates would have been relegated in 1995. And the Clippers would have been gone in 1981–82, sparing Los Angeles this team entirely.

In North America, though, despite years of failure, both teams have been consistently rewarded by their league. The Pirates—via luxury payments from teams like the Yankees—are actually profitable. And the Clippers have routinely been granted high draft choices and—via the intervention of Commissioner David Stern—were recently given the amazing talents of Chris Paul.

The chronic failures of the Pirates and Clippers suggest that the ownership of these teams are less than competent. And in a capitalistic system, incompetence leads to failure. But in North American sports leagues, when incompetence leads to shortfalls in revenue, the league turns to the players and demands wage cuts to compensate the losers.

## Opening All Markets Would Eliminate Labor Disputes

This in turn leads to labor disputes. It's my opinion that all of this could be avoided if losing teams in North America were simply relegated and all markets opened to competition.

For example, let's imagine that multiple basketball leagues were created in North America. Currently, beneath the NBA is the NBA Development League (which could be the Championship League equivalent). Beneath the NBADL, one could create another league. Any city or part of a city (i.e. Long Island in New York could have their own team)—could enter a team in a lower league. If that team was successful it could eventually join the NBA. And the teams that fail in the NBA would be removed.

Such an approach might end the small market vs. large market dispute because the advantages of the large markets—more specifically, the power to monopolize large cities—would end. And without this dispute, maybe the labor disputes that plague North American sports leagues could also end.

Of course, to implement this plan, North American sports leagues would have to end central planning and the desire of guaranteed profits. It is unlikely the owners of North American teams—who clearly profit from the current arrangement—would agree to such a move. In fact, it was reported a few months ago that North American owners would like to end the system of promotion and relegation in the leagues where these owners have invested in Europe.

If these owners were ever successful, then essentially American owners would be exporting central planning to a market-oriented industry in Europe. And who would have guessed this would ever happen?

# 14

# Make the Fans the Owners: A Long-Term Solution for the NFL

*Roger Groves*

*Roger Groves is a law professor at Florida Coastal School of Law.*

*The best way to ensure that players and owners no longer squabble over their shares of league profits while fans are stuck paying increasingly high ticket prices is to make each team a publicly owned enterprise. If fans owned stock in their favorite teams, they would be able to elect a board of directors to oversee team operations and, more importantly, hold them responsible for their treatment of players, fans, and the franchise as a whole. This would force both players and management to focus on not only the accumulation of profits but also their duty to reflect their most loyal supporters' passion and will to succeed.*

While President Obama had meetings with Mexican executives about hundreds of drug-related deaths with US-Mexican implications, someone couldn't resist asking about the potential NFL lockout. His understandably dismissive single-sentence response was that he trusts that these two parties will find a way to share the $9 billion in annual revenue *while being true to the fans* in the process. From a sports perspective, it was a nice change to finally have a single sentence that includes the real object of the affections by the labor combatants. This labor negotiation is not really just about

Roger Groves, "Make the Fans the Owners: A Long-Term Solution for the NFL," *Forbes*, March 6, 2011. Reprinted by Permission of Forbes Media LLC © 2012.

employees vs. employers. This is about how those two factions come together so they can provide a product for the public. The fans are an intended beneficiary of the "joint" enterprise between players and owners. The players and owners have been revenue sharing now for the better part of a half century and always found a way to make it work. But if there were no fans to attend or watch, there would be no stadiums, no TV, and no revenue. And it is well documented that when those private owners want a new stadium, they most often ask the public to buy it.

## The Revenue Comes from the Fans

The $9 billion revenue has come, directly and indirectly, from fans who embrace the sport in ways that make some spouses jealous, lonely or both. Untold sacrifices have been made. Probably some mistakes too—by the average Joe and Josephine that provides fanatical financing of the sport through ticket sales, concessions (both at the stadium and at home), TV viewership. They even spawned new subsidiary industries like fantasy games, and audio and video streaming. None of them exist without the fandom.

The fan's stake in the outcome comes at a price, but not a financial reward for owning the source of the product. So in the country with the most prolific free enterprise system in world history, why not allow the public to buy into the for-profit businesses that generate the game they so passionately believe in? If fans can go on a national market exchange and buy a few shares of Google, why not an NFL team? One offers a search engine, the other offers a sports vehicle. They are both organized primarily for profit. There is nothing in the Constitution, federal, state or local statutes that expressly prohibits it. A reported inquiry has already been made about buying the NY Mets and selling shares publicly, in light of Mets owners having [convicted Ponzi schemer] Bernie Madoff entanglements. The private owners of the Mets were not interested so end of story. The NFL however already has precedent. The Green Bay Packers are the NFL's own poster child for having publicly owned shares, albeit not operating in a classic corporate sense currently.

## Publicly Owned NFL Teams Would Take Fans into Consideration

If each NFL team was a publicly held corporation, any fan could buy his or her "share" of the team. And collectively those fans would elect a board of directors who they believed operated in the interests of the corporation. The current teams are closely held entities, corporations and partnerships primarily. Their shares are owned by a few and you and I have only the choice of paying for the product [and] not owing a piece of it. But what if most fans see current owners as most at fault for blocking the playing of the game? After all, we are facing a lockout by the owners, not a strike by the players. If the fans owned the team, with the ability to elect and defrock the board of directors, I wonder if the board would do more to please the fans who for the most part just want to see quality games.

*Is there anything really so unique about the privately held ownership model that makes it essential to NFL football?*

The prospect presents some interesting issues. Can fandom use a corporate structure to pick executive personnel like other major corporations? Regardless of private or public share ownership, in the end someone has to pick the executives to pick the coaches to pick the players. Having a large number of public shareholders does not prevent this occurrence. Some shareholders in major corporations change daily by the thousands. That does not prevent quality decisions by its board of directors and officers on a daily basis. Arguably, the decision-makers are even more accountable to shareholders because they can be removed if their actions erode public confidence or shareholder confidence in their decisions.

Does the mere fact that the corporate object is football completely change that dynamic? Does the fact that the buying portion of the public is football fans change this time-honored success model? I doubt it. If one is concerned about the volume and conditions for transfers of shares, there are already well-established laws and procedures to restrict the transfer or sale of shares to reasonable conditions devised by the corporation. If the company decided to assure continuity of fans, or prevent the sale of shares to enemy teams, there is a dizzying array of means available to make it happen. Corporations also have a tremendous amount of flexibility on how to structure voting blocks, shareholder agreements, cumulative voting, staggered board elections, and minority shareholder protections. I will be an author of an upcoming book on those very issues.

---

*One wonders if the players would feel the same need to have a union . . . if they knew the owners were the fans.*

---

## Teams Don't Need to Be Privately Owned

And in the grand scheme of things, is there anything really so unique about the privately held ownership model that makes it essential to NFL football? Do we know that the current owners only became owners because they knew more about football than everyone else? No, I think their ownership opportunity has more to do with their acumen in other types of business ventures unrelated to football. Of course it is important to have demonstrated business sense—but that resides among the board of directors as selected by the multitude of shareholders in our largest successful corporations. In the scheme of corporate enterprises, NFL entities are quite small compared to publicly traded corporations. Smallness can be a good thing but also a limitation. They are only a small sample of successful people who gained a comfort level with other owners as a special club, not because they were uniquely qualified. I am not so sure that among the much larger pool of fandom there are not equally competent business people, whose only failure is in opportunity. And I am not sure the thousands of fans who would invest their precious dollars would have a materially different dynamic of selection than other major corporations. Ordinary Joes and Josephines own plenty of Google stock.

Perhaps fandom shareholders would define the mission differently. Many large corporations have had grassroots *shareholder*-inspired initiatives that resulted in a mix of socially conscious mission-based ventures. They evolved a corporate double bottom line of profits on the one hand, and sincerity to a cause on the other. My mind's eye can see Packer fans clutching their certificate of shares in trembling hands of a playoff game at 2 below zero. I just cannot see them voting to make a few shareholders rich for the sake of profits even if they treat the players badly. Their "Packer-pure" voter bottom line would not allow it. My investment capital says Green Bay does not have a monopoly on such a perspective.

One wonders if the players would feel the same need to have a union to protect their interests if they knew the owners were the fans. It would certainly be uncomfortable to threaten to strike against the very fans you seek to please on the field, and community you serve through your charitable foundation. It would be harder to make a villain out of the entire community for the sake of money. Left without a villain, the players are left to look in the mirror.

## A More Compassionate Ownership

But one also wonders if the players would even be in this hardened position if there was a more compassionate ownership with double bottom line. I suspect that if the only teams in the NFL were teams owned by player-sensitive organizations like the Steelers, and/or a group of fandom shareholders, the issues would not be headed for litigation as I fully expect will occur.

Yes, the corporation would be regulated by the Securities and Exchange Commission. But those rules are designed to help the smaller investor receive reliable investment data absent fraud and misrepresentations from the corporation so they may make informed decisions. Owners would have to provide extensive public disclosure of their finances. I am most fascinated with whether the players would believe more readily that a collection of passionate fans would be better at being honest in sharing revenue and disclosing true profits than a small group of family and financial friends of considerable pre-existing wealth.

Of course, I can think of $9 billion reasons why current privately held ownership groups would not desire going public. That would probably take an Act of Congress or a small market team in desperate need of capital, which still requires League/owner consent. All of those options are fraught with seemingly insurmountable hurdles. But many corporate realities today started with a seemingly far-fetched use of imagination and the audacity and acumen to believe in something beyond the status quo.

# Organizations to Contact

*The editors have compiled the following list of organizations concerned with the issues debated in this book. The descriptions are derived from materials provided by the organizations. All have publications or information available for interested readers. The list was compiled on the date of publication of the present volume; names, addresses, phone and fax numbers, and e-mail and Internet addresses may change. Be aware that many organizations take several weeks or longer to respond to inquiries, so allow as much time as possible.*

**American Federation of Labor and Congress of Industrial Organizations (AFL-CIO)**
815 16th St. NW, Washington, DC 20006
website: www.aflcio.org

The AFL-CIO is a federation of more than fifty national and international unions. It supports workers' desires to form unions so they can bargain collectively with their employers for better working conditions. The federation also supports the political interests of workers by seeking to increase voter turnout and by lobbying state and federal governments to pass pro-worker legislation. The group's website includes a variety of information about the union movement worldwide, workplace issues, legislation and political battles, and the AFL-CIO NOW blog.

**Cato Institute**
1000 Massachusetts Ave. NW, Washington, DC 20001
(202) 842-0200 • fax: (202) 842-3490
website: www.cato.org

The Cato Institute is a public policy research organization dedicated to the principles of individual liberty, limited government, free markets, and peace. The Institute is dedicated to increasing and enhancing the understanding of key public policies and to realistically analyzing their impact on the principles identified above. The Cato Institute publishes many publications, such as the *Cato Journal*, with articles including "Sports Player Drafts and Reserve Systems."

## Major League Baseball (MLB)

245 Park Ave., 31st Floor, New York, NY   10167
(212) 931-7800 • fax: (212) 949-5654
website: www.mlb.com

Major League Baseball (MLB) is the highest level league in baseball, consisting of thirty teams (twenty-nine in the United States and one in Canada). It regulates the sport, negotiates labor agreements, handles marketing and media contracts, and hires umpires.

## Major League Baseball Players Association (MLBPA)

12 East 49th St., 24th Floor, New York, NY   10017
(212) 826-0808 • fax: (212) 752-4378
e-mail: feedback@mlbpa.org
website: http://mlb.mlb.com/pa/index.jsp

The MLBPA, founded in 1953, is the union of all Major League Baseball (MLB) players. It represents these players in collective bargaining with MLB, helps them with grievances and salary arbitration, and serves as the players' group licensing agent.

## Major League Soccer Players Union (MLSPU)

7605 Arlington Rd., Suite 250, Bethesda, MD   20814
(301) 657-3535 • fax: (301) 907-8212
e-mail: info@mlsplayers.org
website: www.mlsplayers.org

Formed in 2003, the MLSPU serves as the exclusive collective bargaining representative for all current players in Major League Soccer. The Union ensures protection of the rights of all MLS Players, while also promoting their best interests. The group's website includes links to resources for players and other interested parties.

**National Basketball Association (NBA)**
645 Fifth Ave., New York, NY   10022
(212) 407-8000 • fax: (212) 832-3861
website: www.nba.com

The NBA is the highest level professional basketball league in North America. It is made up of thirty teams (twenty-nine in the United States and one in Canada). Among its responsibilities are regulating the rules of the game, marketing the sport, and negotiating labor contracts with the players' association (the NBPA).

**National Basketball Players Association (NBPA)**
310 Lenox Ave., New York, NY   10027
(212) 655-0880 • fax: (212) 655-0881
e-mail: info@nbpa.com
website: www.nbpa.org

The NBPA, formed in 1954, is the union for all players in the National Basketball Association (NBA). It represents the players in collective bargaining agreements with the NBA and provides players with other types of support, including assistance with filing grievances.

**National Football League (NFL)**
345 Park Ave., New York, NY   10017
website: www.nfl.com

The NFL, the highest level American football league, consists of thirty-two teams. It regulates the rules of the game as well as team ownership, negotiates labor agreements with the players' union (the NFLPA), and promotes the game of football.

**National Hockey League (NHL)**
1185 Avenue of the Americas, 12th Floor
New York, NY   10036
(212) 789-2000 • fax: (212) 789-2020
website: www.nhl.com

The NHL, one of the four major professional sports leagues in North America, governs professional ice hockey. It consists of thirty teams in the United States and Canada.

## National Hockey League Players' Association (NHLPA)

20 Bay St., Suite 1700, Toronto, ON   M5J 2N8
website: www.nhlpa.com

The NHLPA, founded in 1967, is the union representing all players in the National Hockey League (NHL). It engages in labor negotiations with the NHL and assists players with marketing and licensing.

## NFL Players Association (NFLPA)

1133 20th St. NW, Washington, DC   20036
(202) 756-9100 • fax: (202) 756-9320
website: www.nflplayers.com

The NFLPA is the union representing all players in the National Football League (NFL). It was founded in 1956. It negotiates labor agreements through collective bargaining with the NFL and provides various other types of support to its members.

## Women's National Basketball Association (WNBA)

645 Fifth Ave., New York, NY   10022
(212) 688-9622 • fax: (212) 750-9622
website: www.wnba.com

The WNBA, founded in 1996, consists of twelve teams in the United States. It oversees league operations, engages in labor negotiations with the players' association (the WNBPA), and negotiates marketing and broadcasting agreements. Most WNBA teams share an arena with a men's league (NBA) counterpart.

## Women's National Basketball Players Association (WNBPA)

310 Lenox Ave., New York, NY   10027
(212) 655-0880 • fax: (212) 655-0881

e-mail: info@nbpa.com
website: www.wnbpa.org

The WNBPA represents players in the Women's National Basketball Association. Formed in 1998, it was the first labor union in women's professional sports.

# Bibliography

## Books

Roger D. Blair        *Sports Economics.* New York:
                      Cambridge University Press, 2011.

Frank P. Jozsa Jr.    *American Sports Empire: How the*
                      *Leagues Breed Success.* Westport, CT:
                      Praeger, 2003.

Jonah Keri            *The Extra 2%: How Wall Street*
                      *Strategies Took a Major League*
                      *Baseball Team from Worst to First.*
                      New York: Ballantine Books, 2011.

William S. Kern       *The Economics of Sports.* Kalamazoo,
                      MI: W.E. Upjohn Institute for
                      Employment Research, 2000.

Charles Korr          *The End of Baseball as We Knew It:*
                      *The Players Union, 1960–81.* Urbana:
                      University of Illinois Press, 2002.

Thomas J.             *For Whom the Ball Tolls: A Fan's*
Kruckemeyer           *Guide to Economic Issues in*
                      *Professional and College Sports.*
                      Jefferson City, MO: Kruckemeyer
                      Publishing, 1995.

Michael Oriard        *Brand NFL: Making and Selling*
                      *America's Favorite Sport.* Chapel Hill:
                      University of North Carolina Press,
                      2007.

James P. Quirk        *Hard Ball: The Abuse of Power in Pro*
and Rodney D.         *Team Sports.* Princeton, NJ: Princeton
Fort                  University Press, 1999.

Scott Rosner and Kenneth L. Shropshire
*The Business of Sports.* Sudbury, MA: Jones and Bartlett Publishers, 2004.

Paul C. Weiler
*Leveling the Playing Field: How the Law Can Make Sports Better for Fans.* Cambridge, MA: Harvard University Press, 2000.

## Periodicals and Internet Sources

Kelly Candaele and Peter Dreier
"Where Are the Jocks for Justice? Cultural Changes and Lucrative Endorsements May Explain a Drop in Activism," *Nation*, June 28, 2004.

Rachel Cohen
"NFL, NBA Lockouts for Dummies: A Guide to Labor Issues and Why They're Stuck," *Sunday Gazette-Mail*, July 3, 2011.

Philip Dine
"Labor Struggles Shift to Pro Sports Leagues," *Washington Times*, January 12, 2010.

James Richard Hill and Jason E. Taylor
"Do Professional Sports Unions Fit the Standard Model of Traditional Unionism?," *Journal of Labor Research* Vol. 29, No. 1, 2008.

Chris Isidore
"Players' Pay Doesn't Hit Fans: Blame Capitalism, Not Players Union or Agents, for Rising Price to Go to the Game," *CNN/Money*, April 5, 2002. http://money.cnn.com.

Jonah Keri   "MLB's New CBA Is No Help to Small-Market Clubs," *Grantland*, November 22, 2011. www.grantland.com.

Sally Kohn   "The Super Bowl, Professional Football and Union Busting," FoxNews.com, January 14, 2012. www.foxnews.com.

Allison Linn   "NFL's Millionaires vs. Billionaires: Why Care?," MSNBC.com, March 7, 2011. www.msnbc.msn.com.

D.W. Miller   "Scholars Call a Foul on Pro Sports Leagues," *Chronicle of Higher Education*, October 13, 2000.

Joe Nocera   "A Union Stands Up for Players," *New York Times*, March 5, 2012.

William C. Rhoden   "A Separate Union, of Athletes, for Athletes," *New York Times*, December 8, 2007.

Bob Ryan   "Examining Fehr and Loathing," *Boston Globe*, July 1, 2009.

Amy Shipley   "Why Won't NFL Owners Open Their Books to Players?," *Washington Post*, March 10, 2011.

Andrew Zimbalist "NFL Too Profitable to Risk Losing Such Success to Lockout," *SportsBusiness Daily*, January 31, 2011.

Dave Zirin   "Solidarity with Athletes," *Progressive*, February 2011.

# Index

# N